Reflective Practice Groups for Clergy

Reflective Practice Groups for Clergy:

Offering Pastoral Supervision, Well-Being Support and Spiritual Formation in Community

Peter Madsen Gubi

with
Jan Korris and William West

University of Chester Press
First published 2020
by University of Chester Press
University of Chester
Parkgate Road
Chester CH1 4BJ

Printed and bound in the UK by the
LIS Print Unit
University of Chester
Cover designed by the
LIS Graphics Team
University of Chester

A catalogue record for this book is available
from the British Library

ISBN 978-1-910481-05-9

DEDICATION

Dr. John Stuart Whittaker, B.Sc., M.B., Ch.B., FRCPath., Peter's uncle, who was a highly regarded and well-published NHS pathologist in Manchester, UK, specialising in respiratory pathology and salivary tumours, who sadly passed away from the deadly Covid-19 virus during the writing of this book. Apart from his family, he loved singing in the Hallé Choir, was active in his local Church and walked miles on the Yorkshire Moors;

The Ven. Paul Taylor, retired Archdeacon of Sherborne and a St. Luke's Trustee, whose initiative in introducing Clergy group work to Salisbury Diocese proved to be the forerunner of the present Reflective Practice Group model, about which Jan has written in this book;

The Revd. Cody Coyne, whom William finds inspirational, has a strong commitment to welcoming diversity through active interfaith work, supporting LGBT+ people, including conducting same sex marriages, and attracting people from diverse backgrounds to Sunday worship.

CONTENTS

FOREWORD I

BY THE RT. REV. SARAH GROVES

We tend, as ministers and bishops, to be solo artists. We have our own little patches, or parishes, and are often in unspoken competition with our colleagues in our own Churches and with those of the other denominations around us. We rarely speak honestly to our colleagues and, when one does, there is the terrible fear of being judged for our failures. Our work is so deep and personal to us and, because of this, our egos are very sensitive to criticism. So, we take no counsel or support from others who are often, unknown to us, in the same place as us.

Part of this lies in the models of ministry we try to emulate: the Good Shepherd who is constantly with his sheep and ultimately lays down his life for the sheep; or the Servant who washes the feet of his followers and who may suffer vicariously for them and with them. 'Saved to Serve', regardless of the cost, was certainly the ideal that was expressed in my teenage years.

This book explores the ways that the changes in the 20th and 21st centuries have impacted on ministry and increased the demands on Clergy. The multiple expectations on Clergy now, along with guilt at not fulfilling the role as perfectly as one would wish to, can produce cycles of depression and spiritual dryness, with the ultimate possibility of burnout and loss of faith. This impacts not just on the Clergy, but on their families and the parishes or Churches we serve. It could well be said of Clergy families that "they also serve who only stand and wait".

From reading this book, I believe that Reflective Practice Groups could provide Clergy with support and encouragement, space for theological and spiritual reflection and growth, and a chance in a safe environment to look back and consider reactions, choices and decisions as ministers and priests. This must surely be of benefit to our vocations if we become more self-aware and less frayed shepherds and servants, safeguarding ourselves as well as those we serve.

This book brings together all of the recent research around Reflective Practice Groups in a faith context. The history of reflective practice in the Church is explored and there is a generous section on theological understandings of sharing honestly in community. Jan Korris describes how Reflective Practice Groups can be set up and work; Peter Gubi gathers together the advantages that Reflective Practice Groups can give their participants and also the research about those situations where it may not help. William West's reflections encouraged me as he saw from the outside into the lives of ministers, and recognised how hard most try to be the best they can for those they serve.

I wonder, thinking of how complex the issues of trust, multiple roles and line management are in our Churches, if Reflective Practice Groups could be offered ecumenically so that there is less need to travel to get to a suitable group. In the end, the issues that affect us all as Clergy, are not so very different despite our different denominational backgrounds. I would certainly wish to pursue this within my own denomination.

Maybe listening to each other in reflective practice will help us as ministers and priests to hear again the words of Jesus to us, because he calls those who are weary and heavily laden and promises that he will give us rest, because his yoke is easy and his burden is light, and in him we will find rest for our souls.

Rt. Rev. Sarah Groves, Ep. Fra.
Bishop of the Unitas Fratrum

FOREWORD II
BY THE RT. REV. TIM THORNTON

There are many demands on the time of every one of us. At present, given the peculiar circumstances under which we are living with the Covid-19 pandemic still causing major disruption to our lives, there is even more reason for us to consider how we use our time. As well as there being many demands on all of us, we, each of us also make choices every day about what we believe is important and what we do not.

As a priest, I have always found it strange that of all the caring professions, we do not (yet) have to be in supervision as part of our practice, as it is one of the means by which we can safeguard ourselves. The pressures and demands on Clergy are numerous, various and burdensome. How we choose to address those pressures and how we shape the way we make our choices is very individualistic. This is strange given the essence of the Christian gospel is a call for us to realise our interdependence. Strange also because so much of our life in ordained ministry is about calling others to work together, to worship together, to pray together and to witness together.

I had the privilege of working in the Salisbury diocese when Paul Taylor arrived as Archdeacon and was glad to be part of the process that led to groups for reflective practice being set up then. I also had a part to play in some groups being an essential element in work we did when I was in the diocese of Truro.

I am very grateful to Peter, Jan and William for writing this book. It is a serious and careful study on Reflective Practice Groups, and their use and their limits among Clergy. There is much wisdom and learning displayed in these pages. The research is carefully done and is well presented.

In many ways, it must be obvious that it is good to spend time together reflecting on the pressures and joys of clerical life. Yet, this book is also evidence that it is far from obvious, and the case does need to be made that such groups are both useful and important.

In other professions, as the book makes clear, such groups are used and have been used for some time. Perhaps one of the reasons why this book is so important, and the argument for such groups still needs to be made, is because it is contested among some Clergy whether they see themselves as professionals or not.

As this book says of such groups in the conclusion, "They are also a form of Bonhoeffer's ecclesiology of 'Christ existing as community' as both a form of Church (i.e. Christian community) and as a place that enables and sustains Church to be there for … others, … enabling the facilitation and articulation of limitations, struggles and failures".

I know this book will be a useful resource. I hope it will be a launch pad for many Reflective Practice Groups to be set up, and for Clergy to go on reflecting on who they are, and how they are, and the level of support they both deserve and require.

Rt. Rev. Tim Thornton
Bishop at Lambeth

AUTHORS

Rev. Professor Peter Madsen Gubi, M.A., M.Th., Ph.D., Th.D., D.Min., FRSA, FHEA, is Professor of Counselling and Spiritual Accompaniment at the University of Chester, UK. He is a BACP Senior Accredited Psychotherapist, a BACP Senior Accredited Supervisor, an APSE Senior Accredited Pastoral Supervisor and a Spiritual Director in Private Practice, and Minister of Dukinfield Moravian Church. Peter has researched and published extensively on Reflective Practice Groups for Clergy, and is a strong advocate of Pastoral Supervision for all serving Clergy of any denomination and faith group.

Jan Korris is a BACP Senior Accredited Psychotherapist in Private Practice and the Reflective Practice Group Advisor for St. Luke's Healthcare – a charity that provides well-being services to the Anglican Clergy. Jan has engaged with two-thirds of Church of England dioceses presenting the preventative well-being philosophy to senior teams, running taster sessions on reflective practice for the Clergy and helping to set up ongoing facilitated groups. She also offers resilience and reflective practice training to the ordinands in theological colleges and designs and runs workshops for diocesan conferences. Along with her St. Luke's colleagues, she meets with all new bishops and deans for two hours on their induction programme to encourage them to focus upon their own well-being as well as the requirements of their pending responsibilities.

Professor William West, M.A., Ph.D., FBACP, FHEA, is Visiting Professor in Counselling at the University of Chester, UK, and formerly a Reader in Counselling Studies and an Honorary Senior Research Fellow at the University of Manchester, UK. He has been a Counsellor Trainer and researcher for over 30 years, and (among other things) facilitates Reflective Practice Groups for Clergy.

INTRODUCTION

Peter Madsen Gubi

This book is written to bring together research into, and experience of, the practicalities, benefits, limitations, and ways of thinking theologically and pedagogically about Reflective Practice Groups for Clergy. This book promotes the value of Reflective Practice Groups for Clergy as providing opportunity for enhancing their well-being, theological development, Pastoral Supervision and spiritual formation in community.

What are Reflective Practice Groups for Clergy?

Reflective Practice Groups for Clergy are non-directive, closed groups, that aim to offer opportunities for reflection on interactions, processes and dynamics from participants' ministries and personal lives, which impact on a person's ministry. They provide a safe and trustworthy space in which reflectivity can take place at a practical, psychological, relational, formational, spiritual and theological level (Gubi, 2011). They create communities of practice for intentional reflection on participants' ministries (Braudaway-Bauman, 2012). They give opportunity for openness and honesty before others. Participants are required to work towards finding a way to both hold vulnerability and affirm the confidence and authority of the other. They provide a chance for participants to tell their story, to give and receive support and encouragement in the situation in which each incumbent finds him/herself, which can be taken back into the life and ministry of each member. Reflective Practice Groups provide both a learning environment where new psychological skills can be gained and they also model a particular way of attending to

1

people's unique situational needs. This model can be taken out from the group and used in ministry, particularly in ministry to those unfamiliar with the traditional Church and its culture (Travis, 2008, pp. 128–129).

The positioning of the contributors
This book is the result of collaboration between Jan Korris, William West and Peter Madsen Gubi. Jan brings her considerable experience of advocating, promoting, setting up and facilitating many Reflective Practice Groups for Clergy within various Church of England dioceses over many years. William brings to the book reflections on his 'hands-on' experience of facilitating a Reflective Practice Group for Clergy in a Church of England diocese, and Peter brings considerable years of research and publishing in this area of inquiry, and his lived experience of some years in hands-on pastoral ministry. All three of us have a Counselling/Psychotherapy background – of which some who read this book will be suspicious as some Clergy fear any perception of the psychologisation of ministry and theology – and we are all Christian: Jan identifies as a spiritual pilgrim with roots in the Anglican tradition; William identifies as a Unitarian who has Quaker leanings; and Peter identifies as a Moravian who has eclectic, contemplative leanings.

All three of us believe that it is ethical and best practice for all of those who are involved in pastoral care to receive both training and ongoing support, in order to be sustained in the work, so as to provide safe and creative ministry. We believe that Reflective Practice Groups are *one* important way of providing a shared space where practice can be explored, affirmed, sensitively-challenged and celebrated. The call to the priesthood is a call to a life of relationship, but with parishioners and colleagues, the dynamics can sometimes be complex, e.g. there can sometimes be an imbalance and abuse of power which can lead to bullying and/or defensive behaviour, and within pastoral ministry, boundaries can become inappropriately blurred which can lead to difficult situations. This can feel particularly difficult in the context of faith settings, as these kinds of situations represent the antithesis of what the gospel is about and the fruits of the spirit which are supposed to define the characteristics of Christians, and yet the Church is filled with flawed beings who live out their wounded humanity. We believe that Clergy both deserve, and need, a space to take and explore such issues safely. Indeed, we shall argue that it is a theological imperative. We think that if those who are working in far more boundaried settings acknowledge that experienced and trained support is essential to their practice, then the Church would do well to offer Clergy something of a similar quality. Reflective Practice Groups are one of a number of relevant forms of support for ministerial practice.

What is in this book
In Chapter One, Jan and Peter will look at some of the similar types of groups that have been attempted before in the wider Christian Church, and will examine how Reflective Practice Groups for Clergy in the Church of England have evolved. They will also explore how Reflective Practice Groups can be understood as a form of Pastoral Supervision. In Chapter Two, Jan will share her experience of setting up, facilitating and participating in Reflective Practice Groups for Clergy. In Chapter Three, Jan and Peter will explore the need for Reflective Practice Groups as a form of Clergy support. They will demonstrate

that Reflective Practice Groups are a cost-effective means of responding to the Church's duty of care for Clergy in a litigious society, and Peter will draw on his published research to extol the benefits of Reflective Practice Groups for Clergy as a way of enhancing the psychological and spiritual well-being of Clergy. In Chapter Four, Peter will explore ways in which the dynamics of Reflective Practice Groups can be understood theologically, integrating the theological views of facilitators of, and participants in, such groups. In Chapter Five, Peter will explore, through a pedagogical lens, how Reflective Practice Groups can be used to develop reflexivity and spiritual awareness in theological training and spiritual formation. In Chapter Six, Peter will draw on his research to explore the limitations and more negative effects of Reflective Practice Groups for Clergy, and in Chapter Seven, William will offer his reflections on his experience of facilitating a Reflective Practice Group for Clergy.

For whom this book is intended
This book is intended for Bishops, Diocesan managers, Church funders, Theological Educators, Counsellors and Psychotherapists, Pastoral Supervisors, Clergy in pastoral ministry who want to know more about Reflective Practice Groups, potential and current facilitators, Practical Theologians, Mental Health Workers, Chaplains, Counsellors and Psychotherapists. We hope that each will find some useful advice, and ways of thinking and operating, from the content. Much of the research and promotion of Reflective Practice Groups for Clergy, in the UK, has been within the Church of England, and so this book very much reflects that context. However, the principles and practicalities which inform this book are

Introduction

equally applicable across other Christian denominations and across other faiths. Indeed, it would be fascinating to facilitate Reflective Practice Groups for Clergy on an inter-faith and/or inter-denominational basis – but that is for another day and is not the focus of this book.

CHAPTER ONE:
SETTING THE SCENE
Peter Madsen Gubi and Jan Korris

Introduction

In this Chapter, Jan and Peter will explore the use of small groups in the history of the Church, and the historical use of Reflective Practice Groups as a form of Clergy support in the Church of England. We will also explore how Reflective Practice Groups can be understood as a form of Pastoral Supervision.

The historical use of Reflective Practice Groups in the wider Christian Church

Reflective Practice Groups, in various formats, are not a modern phenomenon (Bunton, 2001). Peter has stated elsewhere (Gubi, 2011), that long before any theoretical and psychological attempt to understand the value and function of small groups within his own Moravian tradition, Count Nikolaus Ludwig van Zinzendorf had some instinctive sense of the value of small Reflective Practice Groups, which he called 'Bands'. In 1727, Zinzendorf began the use of 'Bands' [*Banden*] to support the spiritual and interpersonal life of the Herrnhut community. Each Band was facilitated by a person who assumed primary responsibility for the pastoral care of the participants in the Band. The quotation below is a description by Zinzendorf dated 1745:

> That we meet as Bands with each other, that we confess one to the other the state of the heart and diverse imperfections, is not done in order to consult with our brothers and sisters because we could not get along without the counsel of a brother or sister. Rather it is

done that one may see the rightness of the heart. By that we learn to trust one another; by that no brother or sister thinks all the other that things are going well with some if they are really going poorly. Then no one can imagine that the brother or sister feels well when they are in pain. That's why you talk to each other, why you unburden your hearts, so that you can constantly rely on each other. (cited in Freeman, 1998, pp. 259–261)

The following description by Christian David (one of the early Moravian missionaries) shows how these small Reflective Practice Groups were used:

Initially there were among the brothers and sisters several who have a special trust in each other so that they began especially to form an association with the purpose (1) that they want to say to each other everything that they have on their heart and mind; (2) that they want to remind and encourage each other concerning everything they can see or think of each other and yet always to encourage one another to the good in everything; (3) that they want to come together once every week, in the evening, to hold conference or Bands with which they might get to know one another well within and without; (4) that they wish to give each other the freedom for heart, life, and journey, to test and express everything, and so love one another as their own life, to keep watch, pray, struggle and fight for one another, and to bear, spare one another, and help make life easier which is otherwise difficult, and therefore have the community which is proper to the Gospel. (cited in Freeman, 1998, pp. 259–261)

Weinlick (2001, p. 84) states that, "… these groups served as both confessional and means of maintaining discipline and morale". Podmore (1998, p. 31) comments that Zinzendorf's Bands had the "function of the confessional and anticipated to some degree modern group therapy". These groups were focussed on the mutual confession of sin, were voluntary, and were focussed on gaining unmediated grace through a direct encounter by the individual with the Holy Spirit that led to assurance (Watson, 2010, p. 4). They involved being mutually accountable, being transparent with one another so each knew what was really going on in the depth of each other's lives in order to avoid self-deception and search their own hearts more fully – helping each other to see the true state of their own life with God more clearly (p. 13).

Faull (2011), having recently resurrected a research interest in these early Moravian 'Bands', states that "the Moravian method of self-scrutiny and pastoral care was gentle and probing, leading the religious subject to reveal insights about the self and soul, rather than forcing a confession" (p. 4). She argues that the Moravians saw this process as a "walk with God and Jesus", which was very much a process of self-care. "Speaking, investigating, questioning, relating the experiences of the body and soul to a confidante, constitute a central moment in Moravian lives" (Faull, 2011, p. 6). Helpers had to be confidantes of the highest order, with the ability to keep confidences and with the discretion to avoid prying too deeply into the private emotions of individuals. He or she needed tact and a friendly trustworthy demeanour that invited people to open a window to the soul (Faull, 2011, p. 7).

Bunton (2001) suggests that Zinzendorf's *Banden* were influenced by Lutheran cell groups during the radical reformation, and that their use was common in the Pietist movement. In the formation of Methodism, the Wesley brothers emulated the Moravian concept of 'Bands' but added 'outcomes' to their purpose in that they were expected to take people to another level of spiritual development, focussing on 'the right state of the Soul', and consisting of probing spiritual conversations. Watson (2010) states that Methodist Bands were a theological synthesis of Moravian and Anglican piety, in that Wesley "combined the Anglican understanding of mediated grace, through the practice of the means of grace, with the Moravian understanding of unmediated grace, where the Holy Spirit encounters individuals by directly conveying an assurance of forgiveness of sin and their new status as children of God" (p. 31). So, Reflective Practice-type Groups have clearly existed in the Church's history (Bunton, 2001; Watson, 2010) for quite some time.

Small Reflective-type Groups also play a part in the life of some Churches today. Donahue and Robinson (2001) argue for the building of a Church of Small Groups that are authentic and encourage growth in community self-disclosure, care-giving, humility (to serve and be served), truth-telling and affirmation so that "our souls can turn to one another" (pp. 57–71). Nash and Nash (2009) argue for the formation of small groups to facilitate skills for collaborative ministry, and usefully highlight various examples of 'communities of practice' (or small groups) in the Frontier Youth Trust movement; however, their small groups are *agenda-led* and *directive*. Within many evangelical Churches in the UK, and in many Christian communities, small groups (Cell Groups, Home Groups or Care Cells) have historically been utilised from the early Church, and are currently often set up to provide smaller more-personalised groups within a larger de-personalised Church, for the purposes of pastoral care, discipleship, mentoring others into spiritual maturity and Christian leadership; but they are directed, often educational, and agenda-led (McCallum and Lowery, 2012). Heriot (2010) observes that small 'spiritual groups' are coming to define religion in North America. People join them to seek to heal and transform the self, and therefore the world. In them, the search for truth, healing and enlightenment is left up to the individual. Using ethnographic methodology, and from observing five small groups, Heriot (2010) concludes that:

> Meaning-making, when the choices are this enormous, leaves the individual both in control and often alone in decision-making. Diversity, fluidity, and exploration often come with a postmodern price – that is, the community may lack depth, endurance and stability. Pastoral care in such settings is challenging. The caregiver must decide how much to share, to critique, to prod and whether to attempt to influence direction of change at the individual and communal level. (p. 201)

In Singapore, a Centre for Reflexive Theology (CRT) has been created. They believe that it is impossible to be incarnational without being reflective and are committed to listening to the voices of the Other, and to hearing the Other empathetically even when they disagree. They learn how others' perspectives can enrich their own, how to be a listening community, and explore how different people understand and interpret the Bible. While they may not agree with the various perspectives, it is their hope that they appreciate them, and perhaps even use these differing perspectives to enrich their own spiritual journeys (Centre for Reflexive Theology, 2015). Within Quakerism, there exist small reflective groups called 'Clearness Committees', consisting of five or six people, who are invited to congregate on an 'as-and-when basis' for spiritual discernment on an issue of concern (Nash and Nash, 2009).

Within the Moravian Church, there is a renewed interest in some provinces to reintroduce a form of 21st

Century Choir System (Graf, 2012),[1] and Graf (2012, p. 11) suggests that, should they be adopted again, the consequences would be that:

- The individual will develop his or her spiritual relationship with Christ;
- The individual will deepen fellowship with his or her peers;
- The entire congregation will be reinvigorated by small groups of highly motivated Christians.

Graf (2012) has pointed out that the characteristics of growing Churches include an atmosphere of warmth, intimacy and authenticity in which members can rediscover the gift of spiritual discernment and also take risks, and suggests that heart-felt conversations in prayer Bands (or Reflective Practice-type Groups) would help people to look across the aisle and see not a stranger in the pew – but Christ. So, small Reflective Practice-type groups have almost always been a part of the history of several Christian denominations.

The use of Reflective Practice Groups for Clergy support

Reflective Practice Groups have also been part of the support culture of some professions, e.g. doctors (Siegel and Donnelly, 1978), counsellors (Rowell and Benshoff, 2008; Donati and Watts, 2005; Payne, 1999; 2001; Hall, Hall, Harris, Hay, Biddulph, and Duffy, 1999) and Social Workers (Houston, 2015). It is evident from Francis, Robbins and Wulff's research (2013) that, in the USA, *minister peer-groups* have formed part of the coping strategies for reducing

---

[1] 'Bands' later came to be known as 'Choirs' in the 18th-century Moravian Church – neither has anything to do with playing music or singing.

professional burnout among Clergy, with 53% of the Clergy who were randomly surveyed (*n*=744) belonging to a minister peer-support group. Chandler's (2009) research also identifies ministerial support groups as a valuable form of support. Jackson-Jordan (2013), in her systematic literature review, states that peer and mentor relationships are important in preventing Clergy burnout, alongside fostering ways of enabling 'the individual's sense of connectedness with the Transcendent' (p. 3) to prevent spiritual dryness. She concludes that,

> Faith group leaders should develop and fund models of support for clergy that utilize small peer groups and mentors/facilitators ... Faith groups will benefit from the results of such research for designing seminary curriculum and to create leadership development models that can sustain healthy and successful clergy leaders. (p. 4)

Braudaway-Bauman's (2012) article provides anecdotal evidence of the value of Clergy support groups, arguing strongly for external facilitation by a trained group facilitator, and an open agenda. Braudaway-Bauman argues for a 'community of practice' for intentional reflection on the participants' ministries.

> Pastors are helping one another stay connected to the joy of ministry. As they gather together, prayer fills the air, laughter shakes the room, competition flies away, confidence takes deeper root. Conflicts are addressed before they escalate or become entrenched ... Clergy lean on one another and learn together ... Calmer and more generous pastoral spirits are growing in the rich soil of real community. Once pastors experience the transforming power of this community, they can no longer imagine doing ministry without it. For many

years, clergy have told stories about isolation and loneliness of ministry. But a new story is beginning to be told about how clergy find affirmation and support, guidance, and accountability, as they meet in peer groups. (p. 25)

A potted history of Reflective Practice Groups in the Church of England

In the UK, the Church of England has a long history of dipping into group work practice in an attempt to support parish Clergy, but they have often had a lack of rigour and consistency of approach, leading to schemes starting, flourishing and declining, usually for lack of proper 'holding'. The indicators are that Clergy groups have not been sustained for three main reasons:

- changes in senior leadership and sometimes changes in churchmanship in a diocese;
- shifting models of ministry, some taking a more transactional than relational approach;
- and a misunderstanding of group work theory leading to dispensing with the professional facilitators who hold and inform the process.

In the Diocese of Southwark, 'Basic Groups' were established in the late 1960s/early 1970s. They met for one and a half hours for three terms of eight to 10 weeks. These groups were facilitated by two psychotherapists. Group members paid a contribution, but the facilitators were paid an honorarium by the diocese. In 1997, Heather Charlton conducted some collaborative research into what she called 'Consultation and Support Groups' (Charlton, 1997). The unanalysed rich data in her research paper indicates the profound value of these groups to their participants. By

1998, these 'Basic Groups' had changed their name to 'Consultation and Support Groups' in the Diocese of Southwark. They were led by pairs of facilitators who were in regular supervision themselves. The number of groups had grown to 10, consisting of eight members each. They were set up in different parts of the diocese. The purpose of the groups was defined as "to help their members become more effective in their pastoral work and to receive from the group, consultation and support in relation to pastoral situations in which they find themselves ministering" (Walrond-Skinner, n.d.). By 2004, a case was being made for the funding of the Consultation and Support Groups (Bryant, 2004). Their purpose had changed slightly to being a place to "provide support and learning resources for Clergy and lay persons with pastoral roles and tasks and to help members in becoming more effective in their relationships with those they are pastoring", and there were 36 members spread over six groups (Bryant, 2004).

By 1999, the Diocese of Chelmsford was also running similar groups for Clergy which they called 'Clergy Support Groups' (Bagnall, 2000). The rich data from participants, which is appended to Bagnall's paper, indicates the groups were highly valued by participants. In an unpublished Briefing Paper to the Diocese of Salisbury Ministry Development Team (2005), 'Work-Based Learning Groups' were promoted as a way of addressing the isolation and stress that Clergy were feeling, offering them the capacity to feel supported outside of Church authority structures. This Briefing Paper was based on a similar scheme that was run in the Diocese of Chelmsford (2006). This scheme promoted groups as:

- a place of supervision and support which can help to stop the cycle of feeling constantly drained, which leads to a drop in work standards promoting guilt and inadequacy that results in a further drop in standards;
- a place for gaining a sense of well-being within the institutional relationships, within the parish community, within family and self, which will undoubtedly produce a healthier person and priest;
- a place for gaining self-awareness which is necessary in balancing a role in which a priest is called upon to model both authority and vulnerability.

Groups give opportunity for openness and honesty before others and members are required to work towards finding a way to hold vulnerability and affirm the confidence and authority of the other. It is a chance to tell their story – a personal story, a different story, and a valid story. It is an opportunity to give and receive support and encouragement in the situation in which each incumbent finds him/herself, and that can be taken back into the life and ministry of each member.

The Briefing Paper to the Diocese of Salisbury Ministry Development Team (2005) argued for three groups of five Clergy, to run for two years, meeting once a month for two and a half hours with a supervisor/facilitator. As a pilot scheme, it was suggested that an evaluation take place at the end of one year, and again at the end of two years. This was achieved and the experience evaluated after nine months, and two years. The anecdotal results demonstrate the value of the groups as being: gaining different perspective and context; enabling the value of in-depth listening and containing the desire to 'fix' and 'make better'; gaining a shared experience; developing self-awareness; gaining insight into triggers and helping to think of different ways of responding; a place to vent frustrations; developing ways of handling conflict and defusing situations; developing confidence in resisting others' projections (p. 10). The data from this pilot scheme was made available to us, and an analysis was conducted and published (Gubi and Korris, 2015).

In the Briefing Paper to the Diocese of Salisbury Ministry Development Team (2005), there is an acknowledgement that Clergy are poor at self-awareness, at offering compassion to themselves, at differentiating between roles, at asking for support, at maintaining appropriate boundaries, at self-care, and that fragmentation and isolation are endemic among Clergy. This is echoed in Hudson's (2015) article. The main emphasis of these groups was on promoting and supporting Clergy well-being, motivated by a need to foster self-care, self-awareness and support. Currently, the Diocese of Salisbury runs Reflective Practice Groups as part of its Clergy well-being programme. The groups are described as offering: "Encouragement, challenge, insight, wisdom, boundaries and education", and the benefits are described as: "Confidence, change, self-awareness, discernment, containment and group work skills", with the purpose of the groups defined as, "nurturing the well-being of Clergy by reducing isolation and sharing skills and knowledge" (Diocese of Salisbury, 2015, p. 3). The aim of the group is "growth in self-awareness and integration through the exploration of their ministry" (p. 4). It is recommended that these groups utilise an external facilitator from outside of the ordained ministry but who has a good understanding of Clergy life and is actively involved in their own spiritual journey; and that they run once a month, for two and a half hours per month, over a two-year duration.

Within the published research, Reflective Practice-type Groups have also been utilised in the Bristol Diocese of the Church of England, via Balint-style groups to support Clergy (Travis, 2008). Traditionally, Balint Groups were developed in medical contexts, and "work with eight to twelve General Practitioners, processing cases of difficult patients, and using psycho-dynamic insights to explore the patient's presentation and the physician's reaction" (Zeckhausen, 1997, p. 61). They are an ongoing resource for participants, and are not time-limited, consisting largely of 90-minute, weekly meetings that are facilitated by a competent facilitator who is educated in group processes. The format has been adopted for use in supporting Clergy, and Becher (1983), in this context, describes the process as, "Groups of eight to 10 pastors meet under the guidance of a psychoanalyst in order to incorporate psychoanalytic perception into their pastoral work. In studying the unconscious meaning that various situations had for the members of their parishes, the Clergymen themselves undergo processes of psychological transformation leading to changes in their professional practice" (p. 124). In the UK, Travis (2008) evaluated the experience of a Balint-style Group which was started in 2004 in the Bristol Diocese of the Church of England. Although she was both facilitator and researcher (which may have inherent conflicts of interest), Travis nevertheless concludes that:

> … it was a democratically run group where members could bring heartfelt dilemmas and tricky pastoral relationships to responsive colleagues and psychoanalytically trained leaders. It provided, therefore, both a learning environment where new

psychological skills could be picked up, and also modelled a particular way of attending to people's unique situational needs. This model could be taken out from the group and used in ministry, particularly in ministry to those unfamiliar with the traditional church and its culture. (pp. 128–129)

Although the model is fundamentally a psychological one that is run with the primary aim of supporting the psychological well-being of Clergy, Travis (2008) states that the rest of the group agreed with one member when he said he felt that despite the psychological emphasis, "God was in all of it" (pp. 128–129). This type of Balint-style Reflective Practice Group is still practiced in the Diocese of Worcester (2020) today.

At approximately the same time as, but independent of, the Salisbury and Bristol groups, Barrett (2010) set up Reflective Practice Groups in the Exeter Diocese in response to the isolation that she encountered in a significant number of Clergy clients who had accessed counselling with her, but who didn't want to let go of the counselling relationship when the work was completed. Barrett compared her approach to group facilitation with that of Travis (2008) and found it to be less structured and more 'messy',[2] but from an evaluation of the experience, her research found the value of the Reflective Practice Groups to be that of:

- Shared understanding and experience – *'other people who know what it's like'*.
- Sharing common problems.
- Relieving loneliness and isolation of ministry.

---

[2] By 'messy', Barrett means less psychodynamically 'rigid' (i.e. less focussed solely on unconscious process) and more free-flowing and holistic in the exploration of process.

- Valuing the perspective/experience of others.
- A safe space to express/vent feelings/anger and not having to protect anyone.
- Putting things in perspective – alleviating feelings of stress and guilt: *'not just me'*.
- Continuity – the ongoing nature of the groups.
- Trying things out when not sure.
- Humour – as *'a way of letting off steam'* and relieving tension.

With the effect on ministry identified by the participants as:

- Living the Practice – a way of being, thinking, relating, speaking
- Strengthening and building relationships – relieving isolation
- Practising skills – listening, reflection
- Thinking about process – people's experience and relationships
- Responding differently – stepping back and not re-acting
- Courage and confidence to tackle problems
- Delegating more
- More open with colleagues
- Saying 'No'
- Permission to take time out
- Practising reflection with staff team/curates
- Developing different forms of reflecting – journaling – with others
- A step on from counselling – feeling and staying better.

(Barrett, 2010, pp. 102–104)

Barrett's research was conducted with four groups of 13 Reflective Practice Group participants, using a collaborative inquiry method. The research is arguably limited by the unknown, unconscious influences of the 'insider researcher', and the small group sizes (three to four per group). Nonetheless, Barrett's (2010) research offers a useful perspective on the value of Reflective Practice Groups to individuals, and on the influence of Reflective Practice Groups on ministry, from the perspectives of the participants. In the Diocese of Birmingham, Pryce (2014; 2019) set up and researched the value of Reflective Practice Groups as a practical method for theological reflection, using poetry to enable theological reflection. Pryce's research demonstrates another dimension in the use of Reflective Practice Groups in the context of continuing ministerial education.

Following the Salisbury model of Reflective Practice Groups, St. Luke's Healthcare have offered funding, since 2013, for Church of England dioceses to set up Reflective Practice Groups as part of their commitment to building Clergy resilience. This initiative was developed in response to research commissioned by St. Luke's Healthcare, conducted by Christian Research (2013), which highlighted the need for support to be offered to Clergy. In exercising a choice of methods of support that Clergy stated that they would be prepared to access: 49.4% (n=243) of Clergy surveyed (n=492) stated that they would access a "safe environment to offload and discuss issues".

St. Luke's Healthcare (previously St. Luke's Hospital) has a long history of care for Clergy and their families in conventional medical settings. St. Luke's believes it has a respected professional voice with which it can call attention to the significant advantages to the wider Church, individual Clergy and Church communities of providing better support and oversight to those in ministry particularly through normalising Reflective Practice Groups. When St. Luke's promoted its offer of introducing

Reflective Practice Groups into the dioceses, and training on reflective practice in Theological Education Institutes, the value was seen as twofold: putting in prompt help where there was an expressed need by Clergy for greater support, and demonstrating the benefits of Reflective Practice Groups to the senior staff in dioceses. St. Luke's hoped that the Church would recognise the moral imperative for Clergy, and for those whom they serve, of supporting best practice, particularly in the areas of boundaries and safeguarding.

In addition, there are the obvious financial benefits for dioceses of reducing cases of sickness and early retirement related to stress, and the cost of outside interventions such as counselling services and provision of mediation to parishes. In 'The Living Ministry Research Project' (Ministry Division, 2019), participants recognised that there had been no intentional learning on how to promote collaborative working and leadership and that reflective practice, 'learning on the job', was key if Clergy were going to thrive.

Since its inception, to date, St. Luke's Reflective Practice Groups project has helped dioceses to create 36 Reflective Practice Groups (consisting of 180 Clergy), meeting monthly for two years. Currently, 18 more are in the planning process. St. Luke's believes that its position as an independent charity, operating outside diocesan structures, has proved an asset in giving confidence about the confidentiality and competence of Reflective Practice Groups.

The 'Covenant for Clergy Care and Well-being' (Ministry Division, 2019), which was made an Act of Synod in February, 2020, has as its first recommendation a proposal that the Church of England take the initial steps towards, "establishing a culture where some form of nonmanagerial pastoral supervision becomes accepted practice rather than the exception." St. Luke's believes that this recommendation can be used as a lever to ensure that reflective practice remains in the forefront of the Church's mind. The intention is for dioceses, over time, to take up Reflective Practice Groups as a preventative measure to the benefit of Clergy, especially as most Clergy, who have experienced Reflective Practice Groups, enthusiastically embrace them (see Chapter 2).

Reflective Practice Groups as a form of group Pastoral Supervision

There is a growing recognition within several Christian denominations in the UK, and within the published research (e.g. Hudson, 2015), that pastoral ministry is increasingly complex, isolating and 'messy' (lacking clear boundaries which can cause misunderstandings and create risk). Issues within society have become more complicated, there is less willingness to 'believe' in and more apathy shown towards the Christian faith, and consequently Church attendance has fallen in many places leading to demoralisation. There is also little training offered in theological colleges to prepare ministers for what they may face in pastoral work (Gubi, 2019). As a consequence, there are high rates of Clergy stress and isolation; and past-case reviews are highlighting occurrences of poor boundary-keeping, unwise decision-making, and spiritual and sexual abuse (Mullally, 2017).

As a way of responding to these issues, several denominations in the UK, e.g. the Methodist Church, the Church of England, the United Reformed Church, the Moravian Church and the Baptist Church, have considered (or are currently considering) Pastoral Supervision as a way of providing support – and being 'seen' to provide support – for their Clergy. Pastoral Supervision has been defined as

> a relationship between two or more disciples who meet to consider the ministry of one or more of them in an intentional and disciplined way. Such an arrangement allows each person being supervised to give an account of their work, to explore their responses, review their aims and develop their strategies and skills. Pastoral supervision is practised for the sake of the supervisee, providing a space in which their well-being, growth and development are taken seriously, and for the sake of those among whom the supervisee works, providing a realistic point of accountability within the body of Christ for their work as chaplains, local church ministers, spiritual directors, pastoral counsellors or youth workers. (Leach and Paterson, 2015, p. 1)

Pastoral Supervision is an exploratory and reflective process in which one or more ministry practitioners meet together with a *trained, resourced and approved supervisor/facilitator* to reflect on their vocation and practice. The intention of such regular and focussed reflection on practice is to support a change of culture in the life of the Church from one which is often one of isolated and vulnerable practice, to one of support and more safety for ministers, and for those amongst whom they work. *Pastoral supervision is not performance management nor ministerial oversight.* The Methodist Church's policy of 'Responsible Grace: Supervising in the Methodist Church' (2017) states that Pastoral Supervision has three main functions:

- to support the minister in their vocation and practice and its development;

- to safeguard the interests of those amongst whom ministry is practised, including those of children and vulnerable adults;
- to ensure that the ministry offered in the name of the denomination is collegially and accountably reflected upon in the light of God's mission and the purposes of the Church.

'Responsible Grace' (Methodist Church, 2017) states that effective supervision in this context rests on three pillars:

Normative:
- shared theological reflection on the practices and vocation of ministry;
- the shared identification of risks to self and others and the identification of steps to ameliorate those risks.

Formative:
- support for lifelong learning, formation and development in ministry through shared reflection;
- the exploration of creative approaches to demanding issues of ministry and relationships as they arise.

Restorative:
- ensuring that the vocation and work of the minister is shared, valued and nurtured;
- ensuring that health and well-being issues for ministers are addressed.

Over time, a series of Pastoral Supervision sessions should provide for rounded attention to the whole ministry practice of the supervisee(s) including:

- the vocation and vision of ministry of the practitioner;
- the Minister's aims and priorities in the ministry context;
- key relationships in the ministry context and the Minister's approach to them;

24

- the health, resilience and well-being of the Minister;
- equality and diversity issues;
- learning, development and support needs.

All of these areas of attention are equally applicable in Reflective Practice Groups. It is not the purpose of this book to focus on Pastoral Supervision, except to suggest that Reflective Practice Groups are a good way of offering Pastoral Supervision in community. For more about Pastoral Supervision, we refer you to Leach and Paterson's (2015) excellent handbook on Pastoral Supervision. Reflective Practice Groups can be a cost-effective alternative to individual Pastoral Supervision. Although less time is given to the issues that each person brings to the Reflective Practice Group, than they would receive in individual Pastoral Supervision, and although a Reflective Practice Group may be a less honest space (depending on the dynamics of the group), arguably greater gain can be had from sharing in each other's experiences in a Reflective Practice Group, which is less present in individual Pastoral Supervision. In both forms of Pastoral Supervision, much of what is gained will depend on the trust and relationships that are formed between facilitator(s) and participant(s), and between the participants themselves.

Summary
In this Chapter, we have demonstrated that Reflective Practice Groups are not new to the Christian Church, and certainly not new to the Church of England. They provide an opportunity to offer Pastoral Supervision in community. So, what are the practicalities in setting up and facilitating a Reflective Practice Group?

CHAPTER TWO

THE PRACTICALITIES OF SETTING UP, FACILITATING AND EVALUATING REFLECTIVE PRACTICE GROUPS

Jan Korris

Introduction

In this Chapter, Jan will draw on her considerable experience of setting up, facilitating and evaluating Reflective Practice Groups, to highlight some of the practical issues involved. The voices of some Reflective Practice Group participants, gained from group evaluations, are indicated in italics to give greater authenticity to the text.

Reflective Practice Groups can be usefully developed as part of Continuing Ministerial Development (CMD) provision for Clergy and can be promoted and encouraged in the context of supporting Clergy in their professional development. They are based on the premise that Clergy, along with all other professionals involved with pastoral care, need to develop skills as reflective practitioners in order that they have increased potential to analyse context and action, and so improve and strengthen their practice.

There is evidence that this process happens (e.g. Gubi, 2016; Gubi, 2020; Gubi and Korris, 2015) when practitioners work together regularly on their actual issues in the context of a group, and where professional supervision is part of that group process. In the light of the isolation and the increasing stresses that many Clergy feel in their working life (Hudson, 2015; Stuart-White, Vaughan-Wilson, Eatock, Muskett, and Village, 2018), supervised group working also has the capacity to provide important support outside the authority structures of the Church. This can further help nurture the well-being of the Clergy and so have positive consequences for their effectiveness in ministry. Support and supervision can stop the cycle of feeling constantly drained, which can lead to a drop in work standards, producing guilt and inadequacy.

Gaining a sense of well-being within the institutional relationships, within the parish community, with his/her family and within him/herself, will undoubtedly produce a healthier person and priest. How we are, in a group, often mirrors how we are in other relationships. Gaining this self-awareness is necessary to balancing a role that is called upon to model both authority and vulnerability. It is an opportunity to give and receive support and encouragement in the situation in which each incumbent finds him/herself. The hope is that this experience will be taken back into the life and ministry of each member.

It's directly and indirectly helped me focus on Christ and deepened my faith. It's given me a bigger vision of ministry.

Group work for Clergy: supporting ministry through pastoral care

Exercising pastoral care may be the working out of a philosophical position or religious stance, or just be driven by a sense of human compassion, but the quality of support and encouragement offered can only be as good as the integration of self-knowledge and skills within the carer. The acquisition of skills for pastoral work is notably enhanced by self-awareness, or, alternatively, diminished by a failure of psychological understanding. However, amongst Clergy there is sometimes a lack of recognition, or admission, that their personal and professional lives are intrinsically linked. Perhaps those who become ordained have a misplaced fear that undertaking personal growth is an indulgence, a belief that spiritual development should be enough (i.e. God working through them/or despite them), or a concern about the judgement of colleagues (i.e. that faith should be enough, and that admitting to struggle demonstrates a weakness of faith). Whilst Clergy demonstrate compassion for others, the old saying, "Do as I say, not as I do," is powerfully present. It is hard to imagine them advising others to work so many hours, not to look after themselves, live an unboundaried life and expect their families to take second place.

Experience suggests that Clergy tend towards poor boundary setting. They often inhabit the 'rescuer' position, putting enormous pressure on themselves to solve problems, rather than be a compassionate presence providing the ground from which others discover their strengths and solutions. To simply be, like a human spirit level, bringing into equilibrium what is out of balance within ourselves and between and within others.

The organisation of the Anglican Church presents Clergy with some inherent and significant difficulties in relation to language and boundaries, and these are considered in the section on facilitation. The same or similar issues can occur in other denominations too. The role of Clergy is changing within a fast-moving society. Multi-faith, no-faith, gender, sexuality and a shift in cultural attitudes to authority, are some of the more prominent issues. The job appears less focussed, more diverse, and demands significant management skills. For some, it can feel less than satisfying.

There is a considerable difference between urban and rural ministry. Contrary to public perception, rural Clergy life can be very isolated, caring for numbers of parishes but with a sense of belonging to none. The Clergy can be constantly swapping hats between pastoral carer, spiritual director, professional provider of the services and sacraments of the Church, 'line manager', teacher – the list is endless – and these can all be operating within the same person on the same day! Clergy are expected to inhabit and then change their roles frequently, and are often in receipt of powerful projections.

> *… you learn to listen and reflect back rather than find solutions, and listening brings insights.*

A practical approach

Whilst wearing many hats seems to be the nature of the job, attempts can be made to alleviate some of the fragmentation and to enhance Clergy well-being – and therefore the quality of their pastoral care. Key to this task seems to be making boundaries explicit, and encouraging a greater sense of personal integration. Self-development and support offered via training and ongoing Reflective Practice Groups can be one way of providing this.

Reflective Practice Groups in action

Groups of five or six Clergy meet once a month for two and a half hours at different locations in the diocese. Attendance is expected to take place during the working week and costs, comprising of a minimal fee and travel expenses, be covered by the parish.

Groups Offer	Clergy Gain
Encouragement	Confidence
Challenge	Change
Insight	Self-awareness
Wisdom	Discernment

Boundaries	Containment
Education	Group work skills

The purpose of the groups is defined as nurturing the well-being of Clergy by reducing isolation and sharing skills and knowledge. Key aspects are seen as: firstly, reflecting on practice in order to learn to become a more reflective practitioner and, secondly, to develop group work skills from the experience of working in this way with colleagues and from modelling by a professional facilitator.

Whilst groups for Clergy share similar dynamics and potential for development as those provided for other professionals, there appears to be some variance: for instance, Clergy competitiveness, or the perennial inhabitation of the rescuer role, may enhance or inhibit communication amongst colleagues. Due to the vocation of those involved, philosophy, theory and practice, can be central to discussion and would be expected to inform the personal and professional lives of participants at the deepest level.

Also, there can be a dissonance between what is deemed the benign institution of the Church and the experience of its employees or representatives. Where poor management occurs in the institution, Clergy may express an excessive degree of outrage, anger and distress. Alternatively, the confusion may leave them unable to acknowledge their feelings at all, creating a painful incongruence. Additionally, the language of the institution such as 'mother Church', 'father in God', 'obedience', can sometimes lead to unhelpful projections rather than a healthy development of personal authority and integrated personality.

The aim of Reflective Practice Groups is to enable members to grow in self-awareness and integration through the exploration of their ministry. Sharing in the group involves presentation and discussion of work with a genuine desire to receive feedback and invite other perceptions. Clergy are required to identify and review their goals for development during the two years of the project.

The facilitator's role in Reflective Practice Groups

Reflective Practice Groups are professionally facilitated. The facilitator will help the group members to explore their specific shared experiences as well as attitudes and feelings about the way in which the group is developing. The role is one of modelling good practice, maintaining boundaries for the group, providing a safe space for Clergy to begin to reveal themselves and their work, and to explore their thinking, feelings, successes and disappointments. The task will also be to sensitively challenge practice, personal or professional blind spots and be aware of their organisational 'contracts'.

Facilitation needs to be undertaken by someone who can offer both real and perceived confidentiality. The person needs to be knowledgeable about, and skilled in, group work and have an understanding of the role of the ordained minister, thereby modelling healthy boundaries and reducing, as far as possible, the potential for paranoia. The facilitator's role is, with a clear understanding of the above, to provide a safe container for the group in which trust can develop whilst ensuring sufficient challenge to promote change. S/he should also be able to offer implicit and explicit learning about process, thereby enhancing the members' own group work skills.

Having a professional facilitator is fantastic. It's walking in and seeing someone you don't know and won't see anywhere else. I think that's invaluable. It's the holding role that they have, and the fact that they're external means I've felt freer to talk.

A facilitator will be someone who is able to demonstrate experience of working in a group context. Ideally the applicant will have training in group work, or similar therapeutic training, and have significant experience of facilitating groups. S/he *will be from outside the formal structure of the diocese* so as to be perceived as independent and be able to bring an external and detached perspective to the group content and process.

The facilitator may be from outside the ordained ministry, but s/he will need to have a clear understanding of Clergy life and be actively involved on their own spiritual journey.

Responsibilities of a facilitator
- To establish and facilitate small groups of no more than six that will work together once a month, for two and a half hours, for a two-year duration;
- To ensure that the group meeting place remains safe and secure and that group sessions work within the time allocation;
- To assist group members to understand the purpose and benefits of the group, to assent to the ground rules and keep the group focussed on the task;
- To encourage (and hold themselves) the basic tenets of confidentiality, commitment and anonymity of group members;
- To encourage a sense of trust among group members so that all feel able to participate as they wish,

regardless of differences such as gender, churchmanship, sexuality, race and experience, in an environment that values the contribution, thoughts and feelings of all with equity, respect and fairness;
- To invite group members to reflect upon their personal aspirations and identify areas for change at the beginning of group life and to review these at intervals during the two years;
- To support the group in and through areas of potential conflict;
- To invite the members to monitor if the group is functioning to meet their needs;
- When needed, to signpost those individuals in need of other kinds of support to appropriate services/agencies and to be fully informed as to what/where these are.

The facilitator will meet regularly with their own external, appropriately trained, supervisor and be responsible for the confidentiality and safety of any written material regarding group members and their identity. The facilitator will meet annually with the Reflective Practice Group Co-ordinator for the diocese and the other facilitators for management and professional training purposes.

Knowledge needed
- An understanding of group process and dynamics;
- An understanding of the context of the lives of Clergy working for the Church of England.

Skills needed of a facilitator
- Ability to create a non-threatening environment;
- Leadership and communication skills;

- Ability to work with transferences within the group, and an ability from their own training to manage challenges directed towards themselves;
- Conflict resolution skills;
- Encouraging and enabling skills to develop members' self-confidence;
- Ability to challenge individuals to address unhelpful thinking or patterns of behaviour;
- Offer a good model of group work as an educative function of the group so that members can reproduce this within their work settings.

Terms

- Facilitators are needed for a two-year period, with potential of renewal at the end of the life of each group;
- The facilitator will be required to give six months' notice of not wishing to renew their commitment;
- The Diocese will provide the accommodation for the group meeting;
- The Diocese will pay an hourly fee, supervision costs and travel expenses, to be claimed on a monthly basis.

The following pages provide examples of the documentation needed to set up and run Reflective Practice Groups.

The Practicalities of Reflective Practice Groups

Model Application Form

…………………….. Diocese

Facilitator of Reflective Practice Groups

Name

Address

Telephone no.

Email

D.O.B.

Qualifications

Present Employment

Employment History

Experience as Group Member

Experience as Group Facilitator

Two References (one from a professional colleague)

Write on one page of A4 what you would see to be the essential factors in setting up a new group, establishing a healthy group process, dealing with conflict and encouraging growth and change.

Reflective Practice Groups for Clergy

Model Appointment letter for facilitator

Dear

We are pleased you are joining the Reflective Practice Group Scheme in .... Diocese as a facilitator for group/s commencing at (*venue – time*). We look forward to having you in the team.

I enclose the Policy and Procedure book for the Scheme and the Diocesan Handbook which you may wish to use as a resource manual.

The Reflective Practice Group facilitators meet annually for business and professional development. The next meeting will be (*date, time – venue*).

Please invoice the Diocese for your hourly session fee and travel expenses sending this to the Administrator (*name and contact details*) on a monthly or quarterly basis.

Payment can either be made by cheque or BACS.

Please contact the Reflective Practice Group Co-ordinator (*name*) or the Administrator (*name*) with any queries or concerns. We hope you will find the work fulfilling and enjoy being part of the team.

Model letter to a new group member
from the group facilitator

Dear

I am pleased to welcome you to the Reflective Practice Group at (*place*) commencing (*date*). The group will meet from …… until …… (*time*). I hope it will prove an exciting and fulfilling experience for you.

In our first session a certain amount of business will need to be transacted, but we will also take time to explore members' hopes for the group and plan the beginning of the work together.

Clearly, consistency of attendance and good timekeeping will be key to the security and creativity of the group, and for this reason members should commit to prioritising the group over other everyday demands. If you are unable to attend, or are delayed at any time, please contact me. I will be available on my work line (*tel. no.*) or by email until (*time and day*) preceding each group meeting, otherwise mobile contact (*mobile no.*) is advisable.

I look forward to seeing you.

Facilitators' notes

General thoughts around groups for Clergy
Reflective Practice Groups are for nurturing the well-being of Clergy. They must be practical, usable and designed to meet idiosyncratic and self-identified needs. Reflective practice = effective practice.

Facilitation
This should:
- Demonstrate how to pass skills and knowledge to others without undermining confidence.
- Avoid being the expert, asking open questions.
- See the adventures of choice.
- Make interpretation in the form of a question.
- Show how to be prepared to wait, not knowing.
- Hold models of group process in mind to make sense of events.
- Help members to explore tension and conflict.
- Allow the right to fight.
- Enable repair of breakdowns in communication.
- Help members to reflect on group dynamics and factors that help or hinder process.

Setting up

General
- Invite discussion on hopes and fears, remind members they are here to affirm and consolidate good practice and create a reflective space for further development.

- Make it explicit that you are not the expert, the group is a joint venture in helping each member to discover the richness of their own wisdom.
- Explain that learning can happen by extrapolation from group experience, doing things differently, experiencing and allowing difference, making things explicit, commenting on process.

Contract/commitment document – what does it mean?

- A working agreement.
- The ground rules.
- Contact with the facilitator.
- Individual learning aims.

Comment on the group process

- What each member wants/expects.
- Language, shared and different, needs to make things explicit.
- Each takes responsibility to meet their own needs.

Timekeeping, breaks, poor attendees

- Remind members that there will be a six-month review and a final evaluation.
- Remind members to notify the administrator of their attendance to trigger invoicing.
- Confirm diary dates, ensure your email and telephone details are available.

Confidentiality, for self and others

- What do members need to know about the facilitator?
- What do they need to know about other members?

- What is the facilitator's responsibility?
- Establish "a room that is a refuge of safety".

Thoughts on the use of prayer

The group is prayer, verbal intervention may be counterproductive to the group process, silent reflection at the beginning or end is valuable – but agreed and within the time boundaries.

How to manage anxiety between sessions

- If you are concerned for a group member check their support system and encourage this to be used.
- Ensure your own professional supervision is fully used, and contact the Reflective Practice Group Co-ordinator as required.

Process

- Checking in, group business.
- Update on issues outstanding from last session.
- Agenda building.
- Bids for time, emergency requests, facilitator's business matters.

Group members may need help with:

Thinking about preparing for the presentation

- Present in ways that invite inquiry and change;
- Bring the salient facts, context and feelings;
- Look at what you want from the group today;
- Be open to feedback and then prioritise what is useful;

- Contract, explore, focus and deepen understanding/awareness;
- Create new ideas/plans.

How to explore the material presented
Group members or facilitator to ask questions such as:
- I am wondering what you would like from the group today?
- Where were you in what happened?
- Could you have acted differently?
- Was there any truth in how this person saw you?
- Is this reminiscent of a previous time?
- How would you like to have done things differently?
- How did you feel? What did you hope for? Can you explain further? Use open questions.
- Can you pose what you are saying in the form of a question?
- What would you like from the group having told us this?

The above ways of interacting may be new to Clergy, so the facilitator may need to both model and/or explicitly educate group members.

The facilitator may also:
- Identify a parallel process.
- Debrief the presenter and members, asking such questions as:
  - What did that feel like to you?
  - Is there anything else you would like to say?

Giving feedback

Ensure members give clear, owned, relevant, balanced and specific feedback.

Examples for Session 1

- Invite members to say why they have come;
- What they hope to receive from spending two years in this group;
- What they hope to develop or change in their professional and personal lives by the time it ends.

Summary/review of first and ongoing sessions

- What was valuable for you today?
- Are there identifiable individual learning needs or group maintenance needs?
- Review of the session process, what was helpful and what not?
- Outline the plans/requirements for next time.

Review questions at the end of the first year

We spend our lives in relationship. Internally we are in constant relationship with our body, mind, emotions and spirit and within these we have what are variously called dialogical selves, sub-personalities or just aspects of character.

We have a relationship to the world of animate and inanimate matter, to our fellow human beings and, within all of these, to God. Self-development requires an honest appraisal of the patterns of thought, feelings and behaviour that may impact upon the integrity of our relationships. Group work offers a useful dynamic both to undertake this exploration and to take the risk of change.

As we come towards the end of the first year in the group, I would like you to consider the following questions and be prepared to speak about them at our next meeting.

1) What facilitates the opening up of communication in the group and what closes it down?
2) What have you come to understand better about yourself as a result of being in this group?
3) What insights have you gained into how a group works?
4) What aspect of yourself do you feel impedes your creative ministry and how will you act to implement change?

Any other comments:

Evaluation questions on completing the second year

- What has been the most significant development in your ministry in the past two years and in what way do you feel the group work has influenced this?

Looking at the reasons for coming together, consultation, support, a group work experience, change:

- What has emerged along the way?
- What have we learned about ourselves and groups (perhaps some blind spots, disowned feelings, incongruence, lack of integrity from fear, courage, self-disclosure, challenge, staying with discomfort, trust, commitment or desire for wholeness)?
- What has changed?
- What are the losses?
- What to take forward?

Reflective Practice Group survey (based on Gubi, 2016)
The information you provide in this Survey Form will be anonymous and will be collated with the information from all the participants for analysis. It will be used to assess the value of the Reflective Practice Group and improve the experience for participants in future.

We need every participant in the Reflective Practice Group to complete the Survey Form in order for the results to be meaningful. Please note that it has three sections. We greatly appreciate your time and effort in completing it – *thank you!*

Section 1

The following statements reflect the perceived benefits of Reflective Practice Groups that have been identified through research. Please click on the box that best matches your experience:

(If you want to change your answer, just click again to uncheck the box.)

My Reflective Practice Group has enabled me to:

		Agree	Disagree
1.	Feel supported	☐	☐
2.	Feel less isolated in my ministry	☐	☐
3.	Gain insight into the way I think	☐	☐
4.	Gain insight into my way of being in the world	☐	☐
5.	Gain awareness of how I impact on others	☐	☐
6.	Respect difference better	☐	☐

7. Have a better sense of self-care ☐ ☐

8. Have a better-quality pastoral encounter with others in my ministry ☐ ☐

9. Grow theologically ☐ ☐

10. Interact better with others in my ministry ☐ ☐

11. Grow as a human being ☐ ☐

12. Trust others more ☐ ☐

13. Experience my own vulnerability safely ☐ ☐

14. Negotiate boundaries better in my ministry ☐ ☐

15. Please state if there were any other benefits from your involvement in your Reflective Practice Group

16. Would you recommend joining a Reflective Practice Group to other Clergy?
    YES ☐   NO ☐

17. Please give an example of something that worked particularly well in your Group

18. Please give a specific example of how your involvement in your Reflective Practice Group has helped you to implement a change to an aspect of your ministry or your life

Section 2

The following statements reflect the perceived limitations of Reflective Practice Groups that have been identified through research. Please click on the box that best matches your experience.

I have found that my involvement with my Reflective Practice Group has been held back by:

		Agree	Disagree
1.	My difficulty in committing the time to attend regularly	☐	☐
2.	My difficulty in sharing openly with others	☐	☐
3.	My difficulty in making time to prioritise attendance	☐	☐
4.	Others in the group	☐	☐
5.	The manner of facilitation	☐	☐
6.	The structured nature of the sessions	☐	☐
7.	The unstructured nature of the sessions	☐	☐
8.	The cost	☐	☐
9.	Feeling unsafe	☐	☐

10. Please state if there were any other hindrances to your involvement in your Reflective Practice Group
11. Please state if there were any negative effects on you of your involvement in your Reflective Practice Group
12. Please give an example of something that didn't work well in your Group

Promoting Reflective Practice Groups
Interested Clergy should be invited to attend a taster session which may be held once or twice a year as required. The venues for tasters should vary. They should be run by an experienced facilitator and ideally with a present or past group member. Reflective Practice Groups should be promoted at Induction Days for Clergy entering the diocese.

Training incumbents, and all those who undertake ministerial reviews, should be invited to attend a taster session to enhance their understanding of the potential professional development arising from the groups. IME 7 Clergy should be targeted at the end of their training year.

Reflective Practice Group commitments
There should be:

1) A commitment to regular attendance and to making the group a priority, thereby recognising its significance and value beyond the monthly session to enhance my ministry and personal life. There should be an expectation of prompt communication between group members and the facilitator should there be any cause of a missed session.

2) A commitment to risking the sharing of myself, recognising vulnerability is something to be embraced.

3) A commitment to safety and confidentiality so that trust can develop. This means that any conversation about the group (content or participants) is held within the group – never outside it, even with the facilitator or other group members. There are no exceptions to this. If any member feels otherwise, this is to be raised with the group.

4) A commitment by the facilitator to maintain confidentiality when they meet with others to discuss the work. Process only, not content nor membership of the groups, shall be part of the necessary evaluation of the scheme. When necessary, with the full knowledge of the group, the facilitators will present their evaluation to the diocese.

5) A commitment to respect allowing each other to share as much or as little as desired. However, as the group

has been formed for mutual support, if any participant regularly sits to one side this will be challenged by other members or the facilitator.

6) A decision to withdraw from the group should be raised with the entire group at a meeting and not with any one individual from the group. This should be followed by a subsequent final attendance at the group to enable members to express their farewell thoughts and feelings.

7) Payment of the required minimal session fee of £ (?) six monthly in advance, regardless of attendance.

Defining Group membership

Groups are made up of between four and six Clergy, ideally with a gender and experience balance.

It is preferable not to have members from the same deanery. Where, however, options are limited and this seems unavoidable, potential members must be canvassed for their opinion as to whether they will feel able to fully participate when working with a particular colleague. They may wish to wait and join another group or be prepared to travel outside the deanery if there is a more suitable setting.

Facilitators need to be aware of, and make, boundary issues explicit at all times, and use the 'less than perfect' group work situation as a learning opportunity for Clergy in relation to their own working situations in the parishes and wider Church.

Reflective Practice Group Administrator role description

The Administrator will work with the Reflective Practice Group Co-ordinator to ensure the efficient running of the diocese's Reflective Practice Groups. A key aspect of this work is the keeping of information about group membership and names on the waiting list confidential. Details of Clergy joining a group will be given to the facilitator in advance so that she/he can make appropriate contact and to the Reflective Practice Group Co-ordinator if the member of the Clergy wishes to discuss matters concerning their commitment to the scheme.

The following tasks should be undertaken:

1) Meet annually with the Reflective Practice Group Co-ordinator to review;
2) In agreement with the facilitators, book venues for group meetings a year ahead;
3) Arrange two facilitators' meetings a year;
4) Update the CMD brochure entry;
5) Hold the list of membership of groups and the waiting list;
6) With the Reflective Practice Group Co-ordinator, agree dates, venues and facilitators for taster sessions;
7) Circulate details of taster sessions and collate names for groups;
8) In discussion with the Reflective Practice Group Co-ordinator, define group membership;
9) Send details of new group to facilitator at least a month in advance;
10) Invoice group members six months in advance;
11) Process facilitators' invoices.

Reflective Practice Group Co-ordinator role description
The Reflective Practice Group Co-ordinator, in conjunction with the support of the Administrator, will oversee the operation of the Reflective Practice Group scheme.

1) Keep regular contact with the Administrator and brief senior staff, i.e. CMD Officer as necessary.
2) Take part in interviewing prospective facilitators.
3) Keep links with the facilitators, ensuring they are having ongoing professional supervision. Encourage any group work concerns to be discussed.
4) Attend twice yearly facilitators' meetings.
5) Arrange agenda for these meetings and take and disseminate notes.
6) With the Administrator, be involved in updating documentation on the Reflective Practice Group as necessary.
7) Speak at Induction Days and tasters as required.
8) Meet with the Administrator for an annual review.

Factors influencing the assessment process
A key aspect of Reflective Practice Groups is confidentiality, both in terms of what is said and what happens within the group. The need to preserve this confidentiality is seen as crucial to the success of Reflective Practice Groups and this has profound implications for any assessment process that may be put in place.

There is a need to recognise the different realms of language attendant upon context. Measurement, rooted in goal orientation via identifying cause and effect, belongs in the realm of aims and objectives leading to evaluation. Reflective practice, rather than being task orientated, is a process of developing inner wisdom, involving attention to feelings, intuition and beliefs. Here such concepts as parallel process, transference and projection may arise that do not lend themselves to data collection.

When considering whether a questionnaire could be used to collect data for analysis, it was recognised that any attempt to measure performance by its very nature changes the performance that is the focus of attention. The requirement of Clergy to complete extensive questionnaires or psychometric tests is unlikely to be profitable and indeed might discourage participation. They would also belie the acknowledgment that Reflective Practice Group participation is a post-qualification activity promoted by the employer whilst respecting the judgement of the individual to seek out the resources they need.

Self-assessment
The desire and indeed expectation of Reflective Practice Group attendance is that the participating Clergy will make personal development over the two years. Facilitators naturally address early on, within the context of group discussion, questions about previous experience of groups and of reflective practice, work/life balance, support or otherwise from the diocese, colleagues and laity. Participants are invited to identify areas for development and may be encouraged to keep a Reflective Practice Group journal to embed their practice and create a narrative for themselves of their time in the group. There is a review of the group at the end of a year which focusses both upon group process and the experience of the individual participants. At this point Clergy can be given the self-assessment form for anonymous completion and return to the Reflective Practice Group Co-ordinator at the end of two years. It is fully acknowledged that the process described above is essentially subjective in nature.

A model self-assessment form

Please identify one key area of your practice that you feel has benefitted from attending the Reflective Practice Group.	
Please identify one key area of your practice that you are still looking to develop.	
How relevant to your day-to-day ministry were the Reflective Practice Group meetings you engaged with in the last two years? Circle one only.	Extremely irrelevant Irrelevant Neither irrelevant nor relevant Relevant Extremely relevant
How relevant to the Diocese has your participation in a Reflective Practice Group been over the last two years? Circle one only.	Extremely irrelevant Irrelevant Neither irrelevant nor relevant Relevant Extremely relevant
How much has your understanding of group process increased during your Reflective Practice Group experience? Circle one only.	None Very little Little A lot Hugely
Has your group experience changed the way you operate in groups outside? If so, give an example.	
How would you describe the value of Reflective Practice Group to a colleague?	None Very little Some value Very helpful Extremely beneficial
What resource will you use for your reflective practice in the next two years?	

The Ministerial Development Review

The Ministerial Development Review gives an ideal opportunity for Clergy to comment upon their experience of reflective practice, whether it takes place in a Reflective Practice Group or in another setting. It is essential that a question is formulated on the personal pre-MDR form to prompt Clergy to give thought to where they engage in reflective practice, its context, regularity and perceived value. It is hoped that Clergy participating in a Reflective Practice Group will feel able to give some generalised feedback on their experience. It must be acknowledged that whilst the benefits to the participant Clergy and to the diocese are undoubtedly related, they are not necessarily the same. The former is perhaps a better measure of the value of the Reflective Practice Group in contributing to the well-being of the Clergy, whereas it might be argued that the latter better reflects value if the Reflective Practice Group is seen as primarily about training and the ability to perform the vocation of a priest more effectively.

Establishing the value for the diocese of Clergy Reflective Practice Groups

In answering the question "what qualities do senior staff of a diocese require in the Clergy?", terms such as self-awareness, confidence, boundaried, discerning, skilled, a team player with the ability to change and grow, come to mind. The acquisition of these attributes is likely to reduce Clergy burnout and reduce dysfunctional relationships between colleagues and within parishes that can result in time-consuming and economic cost to the diocese. Reflective practice focusses upon interpersonal change, empowering the individual to alter unproductive thinking and approaches to their work and supporting the development of safe and creative ministry. In using a group for reflective practice, some elements of this come from the modelling of the professional facilitator, commitment to self-care by contracting to meet, experiencing boundaries in the group and having these affirmed in their work, developing listening skills, affirmation, encouragement, a safe place to take risks, challenge, collegiality and extended learning about group dynamics.

Dioceses have a responsibility as employers under the Clergy Terms of Service to support and enhance the well-being of the Clergy. Reflective Practice Groups offer a robust, ongoing provision of care. The diocese can assess the benefits of Reflective Practice Groups by:

a) Acknowledging the extensive body of knowledge held by other caring professions using reflective practice, often called supervision, to develop and maintain skilled and healthy practitioners;

b) Setting up and supporting a professionally recognised group work model;

c) Employing a professional facilitator;

d) Ensuring responsibility for the Reflective Practice Group work is held by a senior colleague, ordained or lay, who understands both the needs of the diocese and the integrity (i.e. the theoretical and theological model) of reflective practice;

e) Employing an external assessor, if desired, to do an annual check on the groups' operation, i.e. attendance, interaction, depth of the work, understanding of the participants of the value and process of reflective practice, etc.;

f) Monitoring the feedback on reflective practice in the Ministerial Development Review;

g) Assessing, over time, whether there is a reduction in mental health issues arising, including burnout, amongst the Clergy;

h) Monitoring whether there is any reduction in the time and cost implications connected to dysfunctional relationships in Clergy teams and parishes that can lead to sickness leave, the need for medication and, at worst, a Clergy Discipline Matter;

i) Monitoring the number of requests from Clergy to join Reflective Practice Groups, recognising this as an acknowledgement of need plus feedback they have received from participating colleagues concerning the value of the experience.

Summary
In this Chapter, Jan has made explicit some of the practical issues in setting up, facilitating and assessing Reflective Practice Groups. So, how do they impact on well-being and what does the research reveal about the benefits of participation?

CHAPTER THREE:

THE BENEFITS OF REFLECTIVE PRACTICE GROUPS FOR CLERGY SUPPORT

Peter Madsen Gubi and Jan Korris

Introduction

In this Chapter, Jan will examine the need for Clergy support and how the Reflective Practice Group might help in offering that support. In doing so, comments gained from evaluation forms will be included in italics. Peter will then explore what the research indicates are the benefits of Reflective Practice Groups. Again, the voice of facilitators will be included in italics to add authenticity to the text.

Why Clergy need support and how Reflective Practice Groups can help

A vocation to ministry is primarily a call to relationship – one of trust and dependency upon God demonstrated by the example in the life of Christ of what it is to be a human being. God became as we are, that we may become as He is. As Whipp (2019) says, "ministry motivated by gratitude for such a relationship offers a means of grace to the whole community" (p. 10), and this is as true in the 21st century as in all previous generations of the priesthood.

It is equally true, however, that there have been significant societal shifts that have impacted on Clergy ministering in a Church faced with decline in social influence and economic stability, and which is prey to potent collective anxieties. In Christian ministry, the patterns of relationship within Church communities are often highly complex and, along with public concern about the integrity of other previously respected professions, priests are not immune to a loss of authority. Indeed, the Church's failure to respond with integrity to a number of safeguarding scandals (Oakley and Humphreys, 2019; Oakley and Kinmond, 2013), has undermined confidence, and it can no longer count on an unquestioning presumption of trustworthiness.

It may be said that the Church's response to these external pressures has focussed to a large extent on governance, finance, mission and methodology, and seems often to be less than relational, failing to recognise and nurture its greatest asset – the Clergy – who faithfully, and with grace, serve their communities. It has been against this backdrop that research into Clergy well-being (e.g. Charlton, Rolph, Francis, Rolph, and Robbins, 2009) indicates increased levels of stress and burnout reported by Clergy, who state feeling undervalued and sometimes tempted to drive the work of ministry through an anxious preoccupation with outcomes. So, whereas many in ordained ministry attest to fulfilment and joy in their calling, there are notable others reporting a low sense of well-being, feeling isolated, accessing counselling for strained personal and ministerial relationships, or requesting psychiatric referral and therapy for mental health issues. There may be a number of reasons for this, only some of which are identified above, and certainly not all can be easily rectified. There is, however, a clear indication, by looking at other vocations to pastoral care, that taking a preventative approach can ameliorate many of the difficulties that arise through the pressure of complex and often emotionally demanding work.

The pastoral care provided by different disciplines or professions, social work, counselling, charities, and social enterprises, has in common developing compassionate, human relationships and offering deep caring responses to some of our most vulnerable and sometimes distressed fellow human beings. Most, if not all, of these secular disciplines recognise that to create and sustain best practice in their work, pastoral carers require ongoing reflection with an experienced and trained 'other'. Other disciplines often describe this reflection as 'supervision', but it is provided in the form of professional and developmental reflection and *not as line-management*.

Parish Clergy are exposed to all the demands experienced by their colleagues in the secular caring professions, but with the additional pressures of wearing multiple hats and having few boundaries. Ministry can attract more introverted characters and there are the dangers of privatised and unaccountable ministries with some Clergy making unhealthy claims to autonomy, rather than recognising the call to agency and collaborative working. Lone-working can also occur due to geography and lack of Clergy colleagues, but in all cases the effect of isolation remains the same (Stuart-White et al., 2018).

In the Methodist Church's Pastoral Supervision policy entitled 'Responsible Grace' (Methodist Church, 2017), Leach states:

> Repeatedly the view was expressed and endorsed in the group that a lot of their energy has been wasted in ministry through festering on their own and worrying about how to respond to challenging situations without the benefit of being able to articulate and detangle them with an attentive other. This festering has in fact obscured the core issues and left ministers struggling to respond at all or respond well.

Also, a defining philosophical difference between ministry and other forms of pastoral care is the expectation of exceeding the limits of a contractual relationship and going the second mile in relationships, and this must, to some extent, involve an element of sacrifice.

> An unduly vivid sense of sacrifice, however, unless sustained by an equally vital experience of transcending grace and mutual generosity, can lead to exhaustion, guilt, and deteriorating personal and vocational identity. (Whipp, 2019, p. 10)

So, the call to sacrifice needs to be balanced with the need to acknowledge human vulnerability and the importance of supporting longevity of ministry. Clergy who are debilitated and overwhelmed by attempting a 24-hour working schedule, must be encouraged to hold in mind the grace present in the Latin roots of the word sacrifice, *sacrum facere* – 'to make sacred'.

The poor psychological well-being of Clergy has been much highlighted by research (e.g. Charlton et al., 2009) and it has elicited concerned response in many denominations. Hudson (2015) states that Clergy often offer a 24-hour service to those in need. Their homes are a point of contact for the homeless and those with mental health issues and addictions. Clergy families are often in the community spotlight in a way that other families are not. Clergy tend to be introverts, so the more social expectations of the work can be challenging. Often, they are faced with unrealistic projections/expectation of others which create significant difficulties if they go unrecognised and, even in the self-aware, the painful experience of sometimes disappointing those they feel called to serve can take its toll. Many Clergy struggle to hold appropriate boundaries and stretch themselves unreasonably; the practical and managerial aspects of the role can limit the space to nurture their own faith. Clergy hold a sense of vocation (call) and mostly are highly motivated, but the pressures can create a lack of congruence between the person and the role. The complexity of establishing boundaries is also present in the tension of forming of close social relationships whilst holding a public role. Even with their fellow Clergy, competitiveness can detract from supportive colleague relationships. This can lead to profound loneliness and isolation (Stuart-White et al., 2018). Whilst these factors make it a greater imperative for the Church to embrace the discipline of Reflective Practice, they are not the primary reason for it. Inherent in the call to ministry is a commitment to personal and spiritual growth, and Reflective Practice Groups offer a valuable resource in the service of this vocation.

The well-being and effectiveness of men and women who have been called to proclaim the Kingdom of God is key to their ministry. Well-*being* for those who minister is not just about keeping themselves well but describes their *be*-ing through their relationship with God, their understanding of themselves and the quality of their encounters with others. Human beings flourish in relationships with others – neurobiologists and theologians alike affirm this core principle of being and becoming (Swinton, 2018).

> This theological conception of life in all its fullness is subtly different from, and deeper than, secular notions of 'well-being'. The 'well-being' or 'wholeness' to which clergy are called is rooted organically in their relationship to God, as branches of the living Vine, flourishing through the abundance of God's grace. In lives that are never less than fully human, we seek a holistic culture of well-being which flows from the

> grace of Christ into all the intricate relationships of the whole baptised people of God. (Whipp, 2019, p. 11)

In thinking about the benefits of Reflective Practice Groups in enhancing Clergy well-being, we need to recognise that there are important practical issues that cannot be addressed, even though Clergy may find relief and a sense of solidarity in talking about related feelings with trusted colleagues. Practical matters that can impinge upon some Clergy's sense of well-being may be their concerns about housing, stipends or pensions, family welfare, children's schooling and their own physical health. In the early days of a Reflective Practice Group, Clergy may express uncertainty about bringing these 'non-work' issues to the group, but the facilitator can reassure them that whatever is significant in their lives is helpfully brought into light. "How", they may say, "does this affect your ministry, and how does your ministry affect this concern you bring?".

In secular settings, workplace competence and skills go a long way to creating a sense of well-being, and for Clergy this is no different. Many Clergy express anxiety about not having had sufficient training in the skills needed 'on the ground'. An example of this might be how to engage and sustain relationships with volunteers. Although the Reflective Practice Group is not set up as an educational resource, it nonetheless becomes a place where Clergy absorb helpful information from their colleagues and where they can be encouraged to try out different ways of working.

The following quotes in support of the value of Reflective Practice Groups to Clergy well-being have been extracted from the anonymous self-assessment feedback forms completed by Clergy at the end of two years. Clergy attending Reflective Practice Groups attest to its collegiality and relief from isolation of their role:

"The Reflective Practice Group has offered a safe space in which to reflect on parish ministry and family life. It has reduced the impact of loneliness that goes with the incumbent role."

"It is a confidential place in which to test ideas and shared experiences. It is a group of colleagues who listen without judging and when asked offer fair and honest comment. It is a place of laughter as well as tears. It is a shared experience that has been invaluable as I have gone about my parish ministry. It has been a great blessing."

"It is an important addition to my support network, particularly as I have no other Clergy colleagues."

Reflective Practice Groups offer help to Clergy in setting and reviewing boundaries related to work and family life, taking days off, retreats and holidays. This is much needed and appreciated. Reflective Practice Groups have a significant role in affirming Clergy in their practice. It has been noted that many are under-confident about their achievements and need permission to take rest and to look after themselves. Boundaries are also key to creating safe relationships in the parish and therefore in safeguarding. The facilitator may use the concept of boundaries, and the understanding of unconscious processes to illuminate the risks involved in a particular pastoral situation and, where necessary, to challenge Clergy behaviour.

"I have introduced some better boundaries for managing the demands of parish life."

"It has helped me to think how I should care for myself and protect my personal time better."

"Boundary setting, looking at anger, developing readiness to think before taking on extra commitments, opportunity to reflect on a very difficult period in ministry, developing better sense of self care and work-/life balance."

"The regular meetings have allowed me to take stock each month of various parts of my life and to ensure I build a sustainable rhythm of reflection and action in the formative years of my parish ministry. Thank you for all that you bring and for your gentle guiding."

One of the greatest demands upon the well-being of Clergy is that of managing the emotional demands of the work without a space to express the related stressors, and this can lead to what is sometimes described as emotional dissonance, with a Clergy acting out their job role but unable to access their authentic feelings. Guarding against displays of public vulnerability is generally appropriate for pastoral carers but, for some Clergy, it has been developed into an art form which puts immense pressure on them and on their relationships. Reflective Practice Groups are designed to offer a well-held space in which Clergy can express and explore their feelings, and discharge pent-up emotion safely.

We thrive and grow, from our earliest development onwards, if we are in the presence of those who genuinely care for us, believe in us, are solid and dependable, and are attuned to help us process and integrate difficult emotions and experiences. (Ison, 2020a, p. 60)

"The Reflective Practice Group is a vital process which offers those in ministry a safe space to explore issues of sadness, conflict, uncertainty (and joy!) with others who are often going through, or have been through, the same or similar experiences."

"We can let off some of our steam, and yet people are not fanning the flame, but are listening."

"I would ordinarily have kept to myself during time of bereavement, but the group was a platform to express my humanity. I felt supported and encouraged."

"Meeting other Clergy in diocese, sharing practice especially around taking funerals, space to unload, complete confidentiality, addressing deepest fears, failures and frustrations, sharing challenges finding new strengths and resolve."

The matters of practice or concern brought for exploration in Reflective Practice Group sessions almost, without exception, are to do with relationships. Clergy's well-being is greatly enhanced by developing greater self-awareness and understanding of others. This is a lifetime's task for most of us! Conflicts between individuals and groups often arise from unrecognised feelings, miscommunication about our human needs and a tendency to apportion blame. Clergy flourish through personal growth and become more able to accept, and be compassionate towards, themselves and others.

As the well-being of Clergy must be directly informed by their faith and spiritual life, these are inherent in the work of Reflective Practice Groups.

There is something about being human as a priest that comes out in Reflective Practice Groups as nowhere else, and it is very precious – the Reflective Practice Group is somehow holding the tension between being human, being Christian and being a priest.

Another said that it helped them focus on Christ and deepened their faith: *"It's given me a bigger vision of ministry."*

Clergy well-being is undoubtedly promoted and supported by working together in a facilitated Reflective Practice Group as is attested to by these quotes above chosen from the many feedback forms. As one Clergyperson wrote to their senior diocesan colleagues:

It's been an incredible blessing from day one. I think Reflective Practice Groups are essential to the well-being and sanity of your Clergy and increase the fruitfulness of their ministry.

Since we began working on this book, our world has been overtaken and dramatically changed by the Covid-19 virus, and this has had a significant impact upon ministerial practice. It has also impacted Clergy in their humanity, as they are equally prone to fears and anxiety for themselves and their families, and the real sense of impotence when being asked to isolate from the communities they love. This can be a physical as well as an emotional experience.

Our understanding of who we are and how we connect as ministers is being shaken, and how we understand the world and God is being challenged. When previously safe assumptions about how we live, what we think and what we experience are thrown up in the air, it feels a scary place to be, in our bodies and emotions as much as in our minds. (Ison, 2020b)

Many Clergy report the pressures of adapting their medium of communication and finding novel ways of practicing liturgy and relaying services. National Church directives are not always attuned to meeting the needs at local level, and Clergy can feel unheard or misunderstood. Virtual communication may work in many areas, but a Clergyperson with four small village Churches can spend all day on the phone in an attempt to offer pastoral care to anxious parishioners. The emotional demands on Clergy of not only conducting many more funerals, but doing so in such difficult circumstances, can take its toll – even on long-serving ministers, whilst the confidence of a new incumbent may be completely undermined by such experience. Clergy are faced with having to act in what must seem like a less than compassionate way, unable to console the dying or the relatives as they normally would, and this may sometimes feel contrary to their sense of calling and beliefs.

> The sense of overwhelm (*from trauma*) can also come from having to receive and handle other people's distress and pain, and to have to keep doing it, while trying to hold our own anxiety and distress. (Ison, 2020b).

With daily briefings from the Government, and regular updates from the National Church, Clergy are well-informed, but they are often faced with interpreting advice and working out how to respond when it sits uncomfortably with their sense of self. Feeling coerced to act against their natural instincts has been a painful experience for some, and Clergy's frustration and dissent has spilled over into the media.

As this national crisis recedes, Clergy will need, more than ever, time to slow down, reflect and recalibrate. Some Clergy will experience Post-Traumatic Stress Disorder and may benefit from counselling. Many will have trusted and wise spiritual directors, but Reflective Practice Groups can provide a confidential setting where feelings can be explored and normalised, understanding that what they are experiencing is perfectly normal in a traumatic and anxiety-provoking situation, and Clergy can be helped to find new ways of 'being Church' in a changed world.

What the research says about the benefits of Reflective Practice Groups for Clergy

There are currently only three published research articles that indicate the benefits of Reflective Practice Groups for Clergy. These are Gubi and Korris (2015), Gubi (2016) and Gubi (2020). Below is a summary of this research which reveal something of the impact of Reflective Practice Groups for Clergy.

In Gubi and Korris (2015), four Reflective Practice Groups were set up as a two-year pilot scheme. Each group consisted of four to five members of the Clergy and was facilitated by a counsellor/psychotherapist with training and experience in group facilitation, and who was independent of the diocese. Each group met monthly, and for a duration of two and a half hours per session, over two years. Participation was voluntary. Care was taken in the make-up of each group to ensure that members would not be from the same deanery/chapter (which is part of the management structure within a Church of England diocese) in order to reduce the likelihood of dual boundaries, and to create an atmosphere of confidentiality, safety and trust where participants could simply be themselves, rather than be influenced by other external (political) dynamics. Participants agreed to commit to regular attendance; to share of themselves (including being vulnerable); to build an environment of safety and confidentiality so that trust could develop; to respect each other; and to pay a minimal fee (to encourage commitment and ownership of the process). The facilitators were paid by the Diocese of Salisbury. After nine months, the experiences of the participants were anonymously evaluated by inviting the participants to individually reflect on how well the group fulfilled the hopes they had expressed for the group in the first session of meeting, and using the following semi-structured questions:

- In what way has the group been of value?
- What have been its least useful aspects?
- In what ways have you learned?

The reflections were written voluntarily by each participant and submitted to one of the researchers. The researchers were keen to hear the participants' existential phenomenology as they reflected on the questions. The data were analysed using interpretative phenomenological analysis (Smith, Flowers, and Larkin, 2009). The evidence from Korris and Gubi (2015) was that Reflective Practice Groups provide:

- a place of learning and support that can help to stop the cycle of feeling constantly drained;
- a place for gaining a sense of well-being within the institutional relationships, within the parish community, within family and self;
- a space for gaining self-awareness which is necessary in balancing a role that is called upon to model both authority and vulnerability;
- opportunity for openness and honesty before others.
- a chance to share their experience, and to feel less alone.
- an opportunity to give and receive support and encouragement in the situation that each incumbent found him/herself, which can be taken back into the life and ministry of each participant.

The research in Gubi (2016) was conducted in two stages using a mixed methods approach. In Stage One, 42 Bishop's Advisors for Pastoral Care and Counselling were emailed to ascertain how many of them facilitated Reflective Practice

Groups, or knew of such groups in their dioceses, and to ask if they could be interviewed if they did. These Bishop's Advisors have responsibility for advising on the provision of mental health care and well-being for the Clergy in their dioceses. Eight Bishop's Advisors (a response rate of 19%) responded to indicate that they facilitate (or have facilitated) Reflective Practice Groups in their dioceses. Semi-structured interviews were set up with the eight respondents. The data were analysed using a thematic analysis (Braun, Clarke, and Rance, 2015). In Stage Two, an online survey, using the research instrument 'Bristol Online Survey', was sent to 64 Reflective Practice Group participants, identified by the Bishop's Advisors of three dioceses, with the permission of each diocese. The participants were asked to agree or disagree with the following statements:

My Reflective Practice Group has enabled me to:

Feel supported;
Feel less isolated in my ministry;
Gain insight into the way I think;
Gain insight into my way of being in the world;
Gain awareness of how I impact on others;
Respect difference better;
Have a better sense of self-care;
Have a better quality of pastoral encounter with others in my ministry;
Grow theologically;
Interact better with others in my ministry;
Grow as a human being;
Trust others more;
Experience my own vulnerability safely;
Negotiate boundaries better in my ministry.

These statements were based on 'statements of benefit' identified in Stage One. The purpose of the statements was to discover if the Reflective Practice Groups' participants experienced the same benefit as the claims that the Bishop's Advisors were making about the value of the groups. Gubi (2016) found that the Bishop's Advisors considered the main purpose of the Reflective Practice Groups to be that of offering psychological support to Clergy. This was identified in the data as: offering support, enabling Clergy to feel less isolated, enabling Clergy to gain an insight into the way that they think and into the impact of their way of being on others. Reflective Practice Groups enabled Clergy to respect difference better, and to gain an improved sense of self-care. They enabled Clergy to engage in a better quality of pastoral encounter with others and to interact better with others in their ministry. They were identified as enabling Clergy to grow as human beings, as enabling trust and vulnerability to be experienced safely, and as enabling Clergy to negotiate boundaries better. The data from the Reflective Practice Groups' participants from all three of the dioceses (see Table 1.) also found the Reflective Practice Groups to be beneficial in helping them to: feel supported, feel less isolated, gain insight and awareness, have better self-care, gain personal growth, experience vulnerability safely and negotiate boundaries in ministry more effectively.

Table 1. Collated statistical data from the online surveys of Diocese 1, 2 and 3 (opposite).

No.	Statement: My Reflective Practice Group has enabled me to:	Diocese 1 Agree		Diocese 1 Disagree		Diocese 2 Agree		Diocese 2 Disagree		Diocese 3 Agree		Diocese 3 Disagree	
		%	n=	%	n=	%	n=	%	n=	%	n=	%	n=
1.	Feel supported	93.3	14	6.7	1	100	7	0	0	100	14	0	0
2.	Feel less isolated in my ministry	93.8	15	6.3	1	100	7	0	0	100	14	0	0
3.	Gain insight into the way I think	93.8	15	6.3	1	100	7	0	0	100	14	0	0
4.	Gain insight into my way of being in the world	75	12	25	4	85.7	6	14.3	1	92.9	13	7.1	1
5.	Gain awareness of how I impact on others	87.5	14	12.5	2	85.7	6	14.3	1	100	13	0	0
6.	Respect difference better	87.5	14	12.5	2	28.6	2	71.4	5	92.9	13	7.1	1
7.	Have a better sense of self-care	81.3	13	18.8	3	83.3	5	16.7	1	92.9	13	7.1	1
8.	Have a better quality of pastoral encounter with others in my ministry	81.2	13	18.8	3	57.1	4	42.9	3	92.9	13	7.1	1
9.	Grow theologically	62.5	10	37.5	6	71.4	5	28.6	2	66.7	8	33.3	4
10.	Interact better with others in my ministry	75	12	25	4	71.4	5	28.6	2	92.9	13	7.1	1
11.	Grow as a human being	75	12	25	4	100	7	0	0	100	14	0	0
12.	Trust others more	62.5	10	37.5	4	50	3	50	3	71.4	10	28.6	4
13.	Experience my own vulnerability safely	87.5	14	12.5	2	100	7	0	0	100	14	0	0
14.	Negotiate boundaries better in my ministry	68.8	11	31.2	5	71.4	5	28.6	2	84.6	11	15.4	2

Gubi (2020) explored the impact, value and limitations of Reflective Practice Groups for Clergy in a Church in Wales diocese. The aims were to explore what participants of Reflective Practice Groups experience as the impact, value and limitations of their groups, and to understand better any implications for delivery of Reflective Practice Groups for Clergy. Two focus groups comprised the participants from two Reflective Practice Groups from a diocese in the Church in Wales were interviewed, and the data analysed using Interpretative Phenomenological Analysis (Smith et al., 2009). Gubi (2020) discovered that the participants of both groups clearly found them to be a valuable experience and self-defined the impact on their ministries as:

- creating more reflective Clergy;
- developing greater wisdom;
- building and gaining affirmed strategies that they could take back into relationships within their parishes;
- enabling a different perspective to be gained on management expectations;
- development of self-preservation strategies for coping with those expectations;
- improvement in practice and relationships within their work;
- improving their priestly skills;
- managing boundaries more appropriately;
- approaching meetings more positively;
- managing situations in more helpful ways;
- and discerning what God may be saying in certain situations.

Summary
This chapter has highlighted the need for Clergy support and examined some of the limited research evidence that

indicates the clear benefits of Reflective Practice Groups in supporting Clergy well-being. The next Chapter will attempt to make sense of the value of, and processes within, Reflective Practice Groups through a theological lens.

CHAPTER FOUR:

THINKING THEOLOGICALLY ABOUT REFLECTIVE PRACTICE GROUPS FOR CLERGY

Peter Madsen Gubi

Introduction

In Chapter Three, it was noted that the research, such as it is, indicates that Reflective Practice Groups are beneficial for increasing clergies' capacities for reflectivity and in offering Clergy support in what is often an isolated role (e.g. Stuart-White et al., 2018; Gubi, 2016; Gubi and Korris, 2015; Barrett, 2010; Travis, 2008). But, how might what happens in Reflective Practice Groups be understood theologically? In attempting to find ways of engaging theologically with Reflective Practice Groups, and what might be happening in them, this Chapter draws on theological insights that are applicable to Pastoral Supervision – which are found in Leach and Paterson (2015). The Chapter then explores the theological views of those who facilitate Reflective Practice Groups and participate in them.

Theological perspectives gained from Pastoral Supervision

> [30] The apostles gathered around Jesus and told him all that they had done and taught. [31] He said to them, "Come away to a deserted place all by yourselves and rest a while." For many were coming and going, and they had no leisure even to eat. [32] And they went away in the boat to a deserted place by themselves. (Mark 6: 30–32) (New Revised Standard Version, NRSV)

As we have previously expressed, the demands of ministry can be great. In these verses, Jesus summons his disciples to himself, and to each other, to share what they had done and taught. He also takes them away from their busyness to be with each other in order to rest for a while. It is within a sense of community (i.e. Jesus gathering together the disciples) that truth about ministry is shared, and that the Body of Christ can discern together who Christ is and what Christ is saying. Leach and Paterson (2015, p. 10) say of this passage that:

> … it is Jesus who is intentional and focussed. Intentionally he makes space to listen to the apostles and provide time for them to rest … We need to set aside particular times when we will relate in particular ways and appoint particular people who can help us to keep our intentions.

Leach and Paterson (2015, p. 217) also stress the importance, from this passage, of being met and fed in community. They also draw theological attention to the passage from Luke 24:13–27 (NRSV):

> 13 Now on that same day, two of them were going to a village called Emmaus, about seven miles from Jerusalem, 14 and talking with each other about all these things that had happened. 15 While they were talking and discussing, Jesus himself came near and went with them, 16 but their eyes were kept from recognizing him. 17 And he said to them, "What are you discussing with each other while you walk along?" They stood still, looking sad. 18 Then one of them, whose name was Cleopas, answered him, "Are you the only stranger in Jerusalem who does not know the things that have taken place there in these days?" 19 He asked them, "What things?" They replied, "The things about Jesus of Nazareth, who was a prophet mighty in deed and word before God and all the people, 20 and how our chief priests and leaders handed him over to be condemned to death and crucified him. 21 But we had hoped that he was the one

to redeem Israel. Yes, and besides all this, it is now the third day since these things took place. [22] Moreover, some women of our group astounded us. They were at the tomb early this morning, [23] and when they did not find his body there, they came back and told us that they had indeed seen a vision of angels who said that he was alive. [24] Some of those who were with us went to the tomb and found it just as the women had said; but they did not see him." [25] Then he said to them, "Oh, how foolish you are, and how slow of heart to believe all that the prophets have declared! [26] Was it not necessary that the Messiah should suffer these things and then enter into his glory?" [27] Then beginning with Moses and all the prophets, he interpreted to them the things about himself in all the scriptures.

Leach and Paterson (2015, p. 36) state that this passage demonstrates the value of coming alongside others in the sharing of their journey. Jesus does not lecture the disciples on what they should think or feel, but simply meets them on the road, puts them – rather than himself – centre-stage, asks about things that matter to them, and establishes sufficient trust for them to unburden their heavy hearts to him. Then their eyes are opened. This process of revelation through accompaniment is found in, and is the purpose of, Reflective Practice Groups.

The passage from John 20:1-9 is also pertinent to Reflective Practice Groups:

[1] Early on the first day of the week, while it was still dark, Mary Magdalene came to the tomb and saw that the stone had been removed from the tomb. [2] So she ran and went to Simon Peter and the other disciple, the one whom Jesus loved, and said to them, "They have taken the Lord out of the tomb, and we do not know where they have laid him." [3] Then Peter and the other disciple

set out and went toward the tomb. [4] The two were running together, but the other disciple outran Peter and reached the tomb first. [5] He bent down to look in and saw the linen wrappings lying there, but he did not go in. [6] Then Simon Peter came, following him, and went into the tomb. He saw the linen wrappings lying there, [7] and the cloth that had been on Jesus' head, not lying with the linen wrappings but rolled up in a place by itself. [8] Then the other disciple, who reached the tomb first, also went in, and he saw and believed; [9] for as yet they did not understand the scripture, that he must rise from the dead. (NRSV)

In this passage, Mary and Peter were willing to be present at the tomb – and they are willing to explore it and make sense of it in so far as they were able to at the time. Leach and Paterson (2015, pp. 63–76) draw attention to the different levels of seeing that emerge from their experiencing in the passage from John. Firstly, they notice (the Greek word '*blepo*' is used) the detail of the situation. Then they wonder (the Greek word '*theoreo*' is used) or theorise, i.e. they try to make sense of the situation; and then from that comes realisation (the Greek word '*horao*' is used). Something of a deeper level emerges from trying to make sense of the situation. All of these processes occur in Reflective Practice Groups as honesty and trust develops.

Theological perspectives gained from facilitators of Reflective Practice Groups

To gain some theological perspectives on Reflective Practice Groups from facilitators and participants, eight Bishop's Advisors for Pastoral Care and Counselling were interviewed. These Bishop's Advisors have responsibility for advising on the provision of mental health care and well-being for the Clergy in their dioceses. The insights that emerged are essentially Trinitarian (both social theorist and classical), and the following reflects on the theological language used by the Bishop's Advisors to make sense of their lived experiencing. Eight themes emerged which have many overlaps, but each focusses on understanding aspects of where God might be in what is happening within the dynamics and purpose of Reflective Practice Groups. The themes that emerged are: *Trinitarian*; *Becoming*; *Community*; *Relational nature of God*; *Incarnational*; *Vulnerability*; *Loving self and neighbour*; and *Eucharistic living*.

Underpinning each of these themes is the theological concept of *perichoresis*. Although *perichoresis* is a theological concept found mostly in Trinitarian theology which attempts an understanding of the nature of the relationship between the 'persons' of the Trinity (i.e. Father, Son and Holy Spirit), and in Incarnational theology to attempt an understanding of the nature of Christ (i.e. Divine and/or Human) (Crisp, 2005), there is very much a sense that 'mutual interpenetration' and *'perichoretic unity'* or *'perichoretic community'* occurs when several individuals (or individual notions) come together as *one* (e.g. one body, one purpose) – as in a Reflective Practice Group context. This can be understood as mere projection (Kilby, 2000) using language from human experience to talk about God, but human language does limit theology, and all theology must be approached with a 'hermeneutic of suspicion' (Bennett, 2013).

I, therefore, want to think here of the language of *perichoresis* as a way of articulating a sub-standard *mirroring* (or distortion of a *parallel process*) of the Divine relationship (Three-in-One), which can be achieved among humans who come together in relationship, as they do in a Reflective Practice Group. As humans, we carry *something of* the divine nature, so we carry *something of* that divine capacity for relationship (Schleiermacher, 1977) – with the proviso that human beings are not God, and thus are not capable of achieving that same level of *perichoresis* within the 'persons' of the Trinity (Kilby, 2000). In a Reflective Practice Group context, participants impact on each other (i.e. experience mutual interpenetration) and 'shape' each other's thinking, and affect each other's psychological state, attitude and behaviour; and in a Reflective Practice Group context, without losing the unique character of each participant (i.e. personhood), participants 'dance' (or interact) together as One group (*person-perichoretic unity*). Although this can be thought to be an abuse of *perichoresis* (Otto, 2001), this notion of mutual interpenetration underpins the following themes, with a variation of focus on what this means in terms of making theological meaning from the lived experience.

Trinitarian
The insights that Schmid (2006) provides on the Trinity are profoundly relevant for theologically understanding the transformative function of Reflective Practice Groups. Schmid (2006) argues that the concept of a triune God (God as communication and community) brings the dialectics of unity and plurality, identity and difference, individuality and community to a new peak of understanding of both God and human beings (p. 5). These include that: we are individual people in a relational structure; God is the foundation of our relationship with each other; God is 'person', and is 'group'; Community is 'unity of' and 'in difference' without mingling; God is a dancing group in love; God is 'I am who is here for you and will be with you'; God is plural (diverse, different) yet One (mutual, collaborative); God is communication and dialogue; the

human person is addressed by God to be God's image and to be included in God's community; the relationship of 'them' as 'One' is the foundation for tolerance, acceptance, dialogue, service and love; Trinity can be understood as participation, equality and plurality; Trinity provides the foundation for a valuing of one's own individuality and identity and it forbids the devaluation of other individualities and identities; Love of the one for the other overcomes the exclusion brought about by individuality; by encountering each other we acknowledge the fundamental 'We' of the Trinity; Trinity can be seen as co-operation arising out of co-existence, co-responding out of co-experiencing, co-creating out of encounter. Each of these can be seen in the way that Reflective Practice Groups operate as a coming together of unique individuals with experiences of journeying, to be 'as-One' in a community of self-exploration and Divine revelation, which enables 'participation in God' (Fiddes, 2000).

> By virtue of their eternal love, they [the divine persons] live in one another to such an extent, and dwell in one another to such an extent, that they are one. (Moltmann, 1981)[3]

Although Volf (1998) argues that this kind of mutual interiority is not possible for humans, this sense of social Trinitarian theology (Moltmann, 1981; McDougall, 2005) does provide useful insights that echo the attitudes and

---

[3] Moltmann (1981, p. 175) suggests that this concept signifies a unity or at-oneness that is constantly created anew through acts of self-giving and receiving among three persons. This is emulated in the relational dynamic present among the participants in Reflective Practice Groups.

characteristics that Reflective Practice Groups must embody in their enabling of each participant. Zizioulas (1985) picks up on this theological perspective by suggesting that community (and therefore Reflective Practice Groups) can be a place where 'logos' (i.e. truth, word) can be revealed through encounter.

> Revelation always unifies existence, through an idea, or a meaning, that is singular and comprehensive, forming a connection between created and uncreated rationality. (p. 77)

Awad (2010) argues that the foundations of Zizioulas' ecclesiological anthropology stem from this identification of 'person' and 'relation'. The relational understanding of *hypostasis* suggests that the human's essence lies not in individual existence, but in interaction with God and creation: the human is not a living 'being' without interrelationship with others. The implications of this understanding appear in Zizioulas' re-definition of salvation. Salvation is not a deliverance of the individual from submission to sin and slavery by gaining chaotic freedom. Rather, salvation is being in the image of God by participating in God's relational personality. Salvation is in becoming a relational creature and realising our being as 'creature in communion'. Only then does one gain a real ontological sense of existence. Salvation is deliverance from individualistic isolation that separates the human from herself, from God and from life in general (p. 5). Whilst this understanding of Trinitarian theology has its critics (e.g. Awad, 2010; Volf, 1998), Zizioulas (1985) does offer a useful contribution to the understanding of the Divine within (i.e. self-awareness) and the Divine purpose that seeks 'to become' and 'to relate' – i.e. to deepen the relationship with

God, self and others, which is the implicit and explicit purpose of Reflective Practice Groups. Gunton (1993) does, however, state that the Spirit makes the triune communion a free *perichoresis*, where the one and the many, being and relationship, person and substance, coincide as one God. Foster, Dahill, Goleman and Wang Tolentino (2006, p. 100) state that

> human encounter with that mystery [of human existence] has often been described as participation in the creative and redemptive activity of God, and is symbolised by notions of salvation, redemption, *tikkun* (the healing of the earth) and *shalom* (the harmony intended in creation).

Applying this thinking to a Reflective Practice Group context, it is the Group, consisting of many, but yet being as One, which enables a form of salvation (i.e. a journey towards wholeness), through enabling a greater sense of healing and transformation to be achieved – although there is always a danger that the life of God is too quickly mapped onto human life. This is not to suggest that a Reflective Practice Group is the only way towards wholeness and healing – it is one way.

Becoming

This Trinitarian recognition of holding diversity in unity, and of recognising personhood both as individual *and* as interdependent, interactive and in communion, was evident in the data – and holding these attributes enabled a sense of 'becoming' through relationship with others and with God. In this process of 'becoming' (or *transformation into that which God intended*), Davies (2013) states that the key point of 'Transformation Theology' is that Christ is real, genuinely shares our time and space, and effects change through the

Holy Spirit. If one is changed, then others are changed also, just as one is transformed by the change in others through Christ.

> Nothing is more personal than this kind of reorientation of life. But it is precisely where my life becomes most personal in this sense of undergoing real change, that I find myself positioned, in unity with others, before God the Triune Creator in Jesus Christ. At the point when I am most me, I find I am most him, or he is most in me, as I am in him … This is an inclusive, life-giving Trinitarian space. I know that others too are with me there, in whom he is and who also are in him, and I know too that it is the world – as it is transformed in him – that is the true source of change in me. (p. 18)

The essence of Transformation Theology, then, is to discern *where Christ is* in any given situation, and it is in the ordinary, as it is constructed theologically, that Davies (2013) argues is "the site of our potential encounter with Christ" (p. 21). That which is transformative does the work of the word 'love' which Davies (2013) argues is fundamentally mysterious within the everyday (p. 22).

Community

This 'Transformation Theology' can form part of the coming together of disparate persons (i.e. community) who have Christ in their midst, and His work as their purpose. Braudaway-Bauman (2012) concludes her article by stating that

> at the centre of Christian life … is a commitment to community and a promise from Jesus that he will show up whenever two or three are gathered in his name. (p. 25)

An emphasis on thinking about the Reflective Practice Group as 'community' was evident in the data, yet theologically emphasised in different ways. For some, the emphasis was on remembering that each is part of a greater whole, which some found comforting.

> *I suppose my theology is that I don't believe God wastes anything – fatherly concept – very open for self-discovery, so that's God and the Holy Spirit at work, you could say. Revealing that which is before. It certainly conveys a sense of, "I'm not just an individual". I've become a clergyman, and this places a huge mantle on me when I get ordained or when I get my first parish. A huge core of responsibility gets dumped on me, and everybody clears off the next day. This is how it may make clergy feel – isolated and alone. But I think we are trying to mirror that you are not alone. You are part of the Body, and this is one place where you might feel the benefit of being part of that Body.* (Bishop's Advisor)

In this quotation, the *perichoresis* (i.e. mutual interpenetration) takes away isolation and provides safety for aspects of the Trinity to be at work. Reflecting the theology of 1 Corinthians 12:12–30, one Bishop's Advisor expressed his/her understanding of the Reflective Practice Group in terms of the 'Body of Christ', emphasising the valuing of difference, where each part is important, and yet part of a whole:

> *We are the body of Christ, so a group seems to be a particularly good way of expressing that and of recognising the different gifts and the different parts – the way the different parts of the body interact with each other and support each other.* (Bishop's Advisor)

Here, the emphasis within the *perichoresis* is on the recognition of difference within the union of the Body. These data also reflect the writing of Bonhoeffer 1954/2015), who emphasised 'community' in the sense of "being-with-each-other and being-for-each-other'" (Green, 1999, p. 125).

Relational nature of God

For other Bishop's Advisors, the emphasis within the *perichoresis,* found in a Reflective Practice Group, reflected more of the relational nature of God which Christians are called to emulate (*imitatio dei*):

> *At best they are reflecting the relational nature of God and I think that is quite important and I take that kind of thinking from Barth – that sort of Trinitarian understanding, sort of relationality of God, and say that we are called to do that; and that that kind of depth of relating in a group mirrors that in some way, and I think that is important.* (Bishop's Advisor)

Rose (2012, pp. 6–8) emphasises that there can be no sense of self without other, for we are created in, and through, relationships. Relationships are needed in order to know more (i.e. gain wisdom and insight) about ourselves and our issues. Others give us confidence in our own self-description. Either through a powerful sense of isolation or a profound connection, absence or presence of another is central to our experiencing. As McFadyen (1990, p. 7) states:

> We become the people we are as our identities are shaped through patterns of communication and response in which we are engaged. We carry the effects of the communication we have received and the responses we have made in the past forward with us into every situation and relationship.

Elsewhere, I have argued the necessity of relationship to the concept of 'becoming' and 'growing' in our potential as people who are made in the image of God (Gubi, 2015). Theologically, this can be seen as relationship enabling "the journey from us to God and from God to us" (Schmid, 2006, p. 8). Rogers (1980) suggests that in order for a person to self-actualise and become that which they are truly capable of being, then an enabling relationship must be present. Although Rogers' work has been criticised by some as being 'individualistic' (e.g. Hurding, 1985), Thorne (2002, p. 10) states that authentic self-actualisation has to be *socially mediated* because we are relational. Therefore, we can only achieve our full potential in the relationship/community – which a Reflective Practice Group can provide. McFadyen (1990) states that:

> the Genesis creation narratives speak of human creation together in God's image in a way that should make impossible any talk of individuals as isolated, individual entities because the narratives affirm that human persons are intrinsically related to one another and to God. (p. 18)

This way of thinking does not deny a person's autonomy and independence, but it acknowledges the freedom on which personal relationships are based, rather than regarding them as being coercive.

> What is distinctive about the human relationship to God in creation is that God's creative and sustaining activity elicits, enables and deserves a free and thankful response. (McFadyen, 1990, p. 19)

McFadyen states that that need for dialogue with God and with each other is a grace, a gift and a 'letting-be'. We can refuse to dialogue with God, but we *cannot not be* in relationship with God. We are called to 'personhood' through relationship with ourselves, with God and with each other. A Reflective Practice Group provides an opportunity, an ethos and a space that is characterised by relationship, a desiring to become-that-which-we-are-capable-of-becoming, a grace, a gift and a letting-be-in-love which is achieved through its non-directiveness, respectfulness, love, authenticity and its acknowledgment of God's presence through attitude, purpose and symbolism (Gubi, 2011). Within this, *perichoresis* can be seen as a form of *nature-perichoresis* where participants are relationally 'making each other' in relationship; sharing attributes of each other within the oneness of the Body – which is the Group.

Incarnational

Another way of theologically understanding the Reflective Practice Group, is as providing an incarnational space, and a place to recognise hope through failure:

> *There are incarnational things that are being done. We are in ministry, and ministry is to do with supporting people, and understanding people, and enabling people, and helping them grow. And we are looking for Christ in them, and they are hopefully finding Christ in us, and the Spirit is working between us, and that's incarnational. If you spend too much time theologising and doing all sorts of really important biblical work which will make your sermons amazing, etc., but you don't do the other work which enables you to understand people, and how to make connections with them, it won't come to very much. I think also these groups do provide people with a lot of challenge and how they deal with challenge. People who want there to be – the sort of people who say at the beginning of the group, "What's the purpose of this group, and what are its aims and objectives? How will we know when they've been achieved?" and all that sort of thing. The open-ended indefinable, intangible benefits are really difficult for them to work with, and yet that is the nature of so much of what we do. And so that's quite a good lesson, and also I think there's a huge sense of failure very often. "This is no good. I am no good.*

I'm not the sort of person to do this. I'm not as good as they are"; and all those insecurities that come up especially more in a group where people listen to each other and think, "... help, I'm not like that. I can't do it". That should enable, if it's properly facilitated and people are safe enough, to express some of that. That should enable an exploration of failure in a non-cerebral way, and it seems to me that that's happily at the root of our Christian theology too. The cross is the ultimate failure, isn't it, in terms of normal human experience and understanding, and yet it's on that, that redemption is based. So, you know, there are all sorts of possible theological spin-offs. (Bishop's Advisor)

Dominian (1998) states that,

Jesus revealed that love and communion among persons are the truth of existence, the meaning of our salvation, the overcoming of sin, and the means by which God is praised. That is what incarnation is. (p. 230)

Williams (2000) states that there are different ways of thinking about incarnation theology. One way is that God became human and thus has shown that human nature can carry the divine glory. This means that God has raised humanity to a new dignity by opening everyone to a share in the fellowship of the body. Williams, though, does not argue that the body should be in harmony – but that difference can be valued in unity, as human community is rooted in the communal existence of the Trinity. The purpose of community is to 'construct' each other's humanity, "bringing each other into the inheritance of power and liberty whose form is defined by Jesus" (Williams, 2000, p. 232). Williams argues that it is the role of the Church to make it easier for people to grow into maturity:

> in which they are free to give to one another and nourish one another, free enough to know that they have the capacity to be involved in re-creating persons. That maturity is substantively possible in encounter with the giving God incarnate in Christ; but the empirical human possibilities of growing in it are to a great extent shaped, even if not fully determined, by what we already belong to, and how. (Williams, 2000, pp. 236–237)

In bringing this about, Williams argues for an attitude of service to be the currency of exchange between believers, for growth into Jesus' Lordship to be able to wash one another's feet, as a welcoming attitude as guests at the same table (p. 232). Nash (2002) states that *kenosis*[4] is a characteristic of incarnational theology. Whilst *kenosis* theology embraces the humanity of Jesus, as opposed to His divinity (and Reflective Practice Groups are a place where participants are encouraged to embrace the fullness of their humanity), some theologians, when writing about *kenosis* (e.g. Mahoney, 2000; Macquarrie, 1974) emphasise the emptying out of 'self' and the embracing of self-denial. Whilst Reflective Practice Groups are a place to fully *embrace* self, and *acknowledge* self, part of their character is as a place where you don't have to strive for status or boast about your achievements. Moltmann (1981) argues that *perichoresis*, as revealed in the Trinity,

---

[4] *Kenosis* is "a joyous, kind and loving attitude that is willing to give up selfish desires and to make sacrifices on behalf of others for the common good and the glory of God, doing this in a generous and creative way, avoiding the pitfall of pride and inspired by the love of God and the gift of grace" (Ellis, 2001, p. 108).

> corresponds to a community in which people are defined through their relations with one another and in their significance for one another, not in opposition to one another, in terms of power and possession. (p. 198)

In that sense, Group members practice a kind of discipline of self-effacement in order to give one another the time they need to talk. Gunton (1997) puts the emphasis in *kenosis* theology on self-denial, on God being able "to empty himself on behalf of that which he is not" (p. 172). Putting that concept in the context of Reflective Practice Groups, in seeking to imitate Christ, through grace, *kenosis* can also be seen in participants using the space to reflect and filter out 'process' that is not theirs' (i.e. which is contaminated by that of others), to enable them to be more fully present to others in their encounters with others. All of these ways of thinking about incarnation underpin the attitudinal qualities to be found in, and purpose of, Reflective Practice Groups. Bonhoeffer (1966) writes of incarnational theology as seeing Christ as "a beggar among beggars, as an outcast among the outcast, despairing among the despairing, dying among the dying" (p. 111) – a Christ whom Christians must imitate (*imitatio dei*).

Vulnerability

Reflective Practice Groups can also be seen as a place where vulnerability can be expressed and accompanied, as Christ partook in vulnerability and in the accompaniment of the vulnerable. This mirrors Kelly's (2014) 'Theology of Presence'. Kelly, writing from within the context of Pastoral Supervision, refers to the development of the embodiment of reflection in practice, and then being able to risk responding and acting with *phronesis* (or practical wisdom).[5] This leads to a theology that embraces risk as we face our vulnerable self. It risks staying with the

> mundane, even the boring, and being familiar with their patterns so that the treasure which points to possible transformation and glimpses of transcendence may be intuited and mined for. (p. 47)

This requires a reflective, embodied self in order to create opportunities for personal and professional growth, characterised by tenderness, gentleness and grace; requiring us to love our neighbours as ourselves (Matthew 22:39) and to give forgiveness to self and others in a co-created safe space, secure in the knowledge that we are loved unconditionally by God (all part of *perichoretic unity*). The embodied, reflexive self is the primary resource to facilitate the promotion of shared vulnerability and real possibilities of learning and transformation.

> *It's an experience of being vulnerable, and if you are going to go into ministry and you are going to be proclaiming a theology, which, after all, is based on vulnerability – because you can't get much more vulnerable than the baby born out of wedlock and made a refugee, etc., or the broken body on the cross. So, your theology is based on vulnerability and strength through vulnerability. It is absolutely no good at all to be immune from experiencing your own vulnerability and defended against it, because how can you possibly walk alongside someone who is?* (Bishop's Advisor)

---

[5] Kelly (2014, p. 41) defines *phronesis* as "being the creative and discerning use of knowledge (including awareness of self) in the moment acquired through ongoing reflective practice and engagement with a relevant evidence base informing practice".

Loving self and neighbour

The love of self, Dominian (1998, p. 10) states, is "possession of oneself which feels good and which is available in service to others". This valuing of self in order to be available in the service of others, and the fact that a Reflective Practice Group is time that is deliberately set apart from the norm of daily life to regenerate 'self', was viewed by one of the Bishop's Advisors as:

> *So, in theological terms, it could be something around the fact that Jesus took himself away from the crowds – the sort of 'love thy neighbour as thyself'. Ministers are very good at attending to others, but not as good at looking after themselves; and it is this thing about, "is it selfish?" "Is it self-indulgent?" And self-care doesn't mean self-denial? So, around that, Jesus took time out to look after himself, to go to set aside time to pray, to be alone, to be with his disciples ... If you've got nothing left to take up your cross with; if you are completely spent, if you are burnt out, then you've got nothing left. Nothing left to give to follow Jesus with. You know, recognising our humanness and our limits, and I don't believe that Jesus meant us to be so depleted and so burnt out that we can't have a ministry if it's so burnt out, depleted. There's nothing left to give and ministry is very much about giving. But if you are not giving to yourself, you've nothing left to give to others. And that's the danger with clergy that are burnt out, and they just work harder but producing less, which is a great sadness, and when they say, "I haven't a prayer life. I'm too busy", there's something really wrong there.* (Bishop's Advisor)

This Bishop's Advisor is expressing the idea of the group providing a place of sustenance in a different way – as reflecting the journey of the disciples in which "*the group represented something about coming to a resource and taking something, and then going out, and it being worked out in practice*", and, making reference to Hebrews 12, as enabling participants to 'run the race' (or undertake the tasks of ministry).

> *This is another way of addressing self-care and sustaining yourself in the ministry. It's a marathon. Where do you get the support that you need so that you can have time out to reflect. Am I sustained sufficiently? Often issues might come up about, "I'm too busy. I haven't time to stop, you know. I haven't a prayer life". So, if that's happening, what's stopping them? So, the group will support each other in that in terms of that useful phrase to reflect and stop when the rest of the time they are just running.* (Bishop's Advisor)

Eucharistic living

One Bishop's Advisor spoke of the ritualistic nature of the group (with its contract and boundaries) as a form of "Eucharistic living" which provides a *"container for discovering more about the Divine through the unconscious"* through which redemption can be gained (again, part of the *perichoretic unity*). As well as the sense of ritual, the Eucharist enables the coming together of individuals in one body as part of a sacred act (another form of *perichoretic unity*) or encounter.

Reflective Practice Group participants' theological reflections

I will close this Chapter with some comments gained from Reflective Practice Group participants:

Growth to fullness

Some participants expressed different ways in which Reflective Practice Groups enable participants to become the person that God intended them to be:

"The honest reflection allows you to develop as an individual to grow to fullness of life."

"It enabled me to reflect on the outworking of my faith and the opportunity to reflect on who I am, and my gifts and faults, was both a humbling and liberating experience. I felt it helped me to be a more grounded, whole, real person."

"That entails bringing more of myself into the light, being more conscious, about discovering the image of God in which I am created – and enabling that true me to live."

One participant expressed that this growth (or becoming) was not always visible to oneself, but that the group enabled a person to see God in that process. This was echoed by another participant:

Allowing others to see God in you even when you can't.

Realise that my God-given gifts have something to benefit others.

Love yourself and your neighbour
The Reflective Practice Group enabled participants at least to begin the process of learning to love themselves, so that they were more able to love others:

I would see it as part of our theological understanding of loving yourself and your neighbour.

God's creation
Reflecting on their lives as God's creation, meant that they were to be valued. The Reflective Practice Group enables nourishment and sustenance in the valuing of that creation:

Theologically, it has reminded me that all aspects of our lives are part of God's creating of us as unique individuals and we can be nourished and sustained in many ways.

The centrality of God

Several participants reflected on the need to keep the centrality of God in focus, in their lives. The Reflective Practice Group provided the space to "come back to God" or "refocus on the things of God". These were expressed as:

> "My ministry is strengthened when I take the time to reflect, pray, do, and review. It helps me to ensure God is at the centre of activity – not ego or number crunching!"

> "The question at the heart of all of our ups and downs has to be where is God in all of this, in the darkness and in the light, in the blessing of new life and the nurture of families experiencing the end of life. Our calling covers the vastness of life and death and work and play and sin and forgiveness and all the other multi-faceted experiences of humankind. Somehow, we are expected to encompass and process it all and find within it the heartbeat of God. This is not humanly possible but reflective practice opens new doors and windows."

Participating in the mission of God as disciples

Preparing themselves, and supporting each other, to participate in God's mission was perceived as a function of the Reflective Practice Group. This was expressed in different ways:

> "Participating in the mission of God, reflecting back to each other something of the image of God that we detect in one another (perhaps offering insights that the individual may not have been able to perceive; speaking the truth in love; offering/receiving a theology of hope and encouragement and building up; sharing one another's burdens, laying down burdens)."

> "... 'confess your sins to one another ...'; ... 'bear one another's burdens ...'; '... telling the truth in love ...'; '... Let each one think of themselves with sober judgement ...'; I Corinthians 12; Hebrews 10:23–25, etc."

"We are all disciples working towards one common purpose. But with a need to support one another through the work we are called to do."

Part of that process involved valuing difference, and the gifts of others:

"I think it mirrors something that the first disciples modelled among themselves in the early church."

"Theologically it enhanced my recognition of the role of female priest and how the Lord uses their ministry."

Community with, and of, God

Finally, the intrinsic need for community with, and of, God was recognised:

"Humanity has been created for community with God and others, and these groups remind us that we are not lonely individuals but part of a greater whole."

"Being held in a loving, non-judgemental space and looking at potentially difficult situations through different lenses allowing light and clarity to come in and transform my behaviour."

Summary

Although, not in any way exhaustive, this Chapter has provided a number of ways of thinking theologically about the purpose of, and what might be happening in, Reflective Practice Groups, which underpin their value. In doing so, the views of facilitators and participants are voiced. So, how might Reflective Practice Groups be of pedagogical value in the training of ordinands, and in spiritual formation?

CHAPTER FIVE:

DEVELOPING REFLECTIVITY AND SPIRITUAL FORMATION IN CLERGY TRAINING THROUGH REFLECTIVE PRACTICE GROUPS

Peter Madsen Gubi

Introduction

Ordination training within the Church of England, and in other denominations, has undergone many changes over the past hundred years (Reiss, 2013). In recent years, it has become increasingly important for ordinands in the Church of England to become reflective practitioners[6] (Church of England, 2014, pp. 10–15). This is bringing about a shift of focus in pre- and post-ordination training, from training for a "professional style of ministry, to training for a more embodied approach to ministerial leadership" (Ladd, 2014, pp. 358–359).

Whilst some (e.g. Ixer, 1999; 2010) may question the 'speculative and conjectural nature' of reflective practice, reflective practice enables the development of one's ability to understand the part that one plays in a situation, and what one brings to an encounter with others, enabling the formation of deeper insight and relationality, and a more developed ability to deal with, and survive, complex

---

[6] Walton (2014, p. xvi) states that the types of questions that reflexive enquirers ask of themselves include: "How does my personal history generate presuppositions that influence my approach to this topic? How does my gender/class/ethnicity/ sexual identity/cultural location influence my understanding? Where do my allegiances lie, and how do my commitments guide my approach to inquiry? What can my body and my emotional responses contribute to generating the knowledge I seek?"

situations – thus enabling better care, quality of encounter and self-care (Walton, 2014). In a ministerial context, reflective practice can enable better preaching (Craddock, 2002), self-care (Burton and Burton, 2009; Lee and Horsman, 2002), pastoral encounters (Kelly, 2012; Lyall, 2009), missional leadership (Diocese of Glasgow and Galloway, 2012) and 'regenerative practice' (Nash, 2011).

Reflectivity is seemingly promoted as a modern phenomenon (Thompson and Thompson, 2008), yet it has long been inherent in a method of theological reflection termed, 'Heart Theology', which "looks to the self and the interior life as the primary space in which theological awareness is generated" (Graham, Walton, and Ward, 2005, p. 18). This form of theological reflection has its roots in the writings of Augustine (Graham, Walton, and Ward 2007, p. 51), and was developed further by the Pietist Movement. Friedrich Schleiermacher (1768–1834) – the father of Practical Theology – was theologically influenced by Heart Theology. In developing his theological paradigm, Schleiermacher highlighted the importance of psychological understanding (i.e. what he called *Divination* – or intuitive perception), alongside the historical study of scriptural text (or *dogmatics*), in the process of hermeneutics, which is "deeply self-involving" and derives from "the passionate human engagement with theology" (Crouter, 2005, p. 124).

The pedagogy utilised to develop interior theological reflection has historically been through autobiographical accounts, letters, journalling, verbatim reports and creative writing (Walton, 2014). Yet, Reflective Practice Group work is also an important pedagogy. Rhymes (1993, pp. 188–193) has argued for the training of ordinands to embrace the formation of small groups, as a form of pedagogy, in which the deepest expressions of humanity can be made and received, "to experience at those times a sense of what might be called 'the beyond in our midst", 'a depth of life', 'a sense of God'' (p. 194). Citing Moltmann (1973, p. 86), Rhymes (1993) states that, "being there for others has as its end to be with others in liberty; being there for others is the way to redemption of life; being there for others is the form which the liberated and redeemed life has taken" (p. 195). Bonhoeffer (1954/2015) also placed great emphasis on Christian community (of which a Reflective Practice Group is one form) and on the importance of each individual in the community (group); on the importance of sharing 'gifts of faith' with others in the community; of discovering about self, others and God; of being with yourself and knowing yourself; and of bearing each other's burdens; and the appropriate place of meekness (e.g. learning sometimes to stay appropriately silent) in community. In developing the concept of 'Lifelong Learning' in ministerial training, Ward (2005) primarily promotes the pedagogy of 'pastoral supervision' as "the place to play and inter-play" theologically. However, much of what Ward argues as being beneficial from that process of Pastoral Supervision is also applicable to the use of Reflective Practice Groups in theological education. Drawing on the work of Taylor (1972), Ward (2005) emphasises the need for a space in which "God is there on the inside of human relating, undergirding the ways in which relatedness between self and other is carried forward without collapsing otherness into the self" (p. 95). This enables differences to be valued, and an opportunity for the Holy Spirit to 'dance around (*perichoresis*)' (p. 97). Ward elaborates on the importance of developing the capacity to listen, to contract, to maintain and develop appropriate boundaries – all of which can be developed in Reflective Practice Groups. In that safe environment, there is the opportunity to experiment, to 'play' theologically and to practice alternative scenarios with others.

Sims (2011) promotes the need for developing a "capacity for reflection" in responding theologically to "the complexity of ministry in an increasingly pluralistic world" (p. 166). Sims, drawing on the works of Schön (1984), and Wolfe and Kolb (1980), places great importance on the 'tacit knowing' that, in the context of Ministry, contributes to a *repertoire* of pastoral responses that spring from the unconscious, and enables a *knowing-in-action*. This *knowing-in-action*, then leads to a *reflection-in-action*, then a *reflection-on-action* and then to a *reflection-for-action*. This, according to Schön (1984), is the process for the reflective practitioner. Sims (2011) argues that engaging in this process keeps vitality alive in ministry and prevents past mistakes from occurring (p. 169). Drawing on Wolfe and Kolb's (1980) Learning Cycle, *but adding a theological perspective*, Sims (2011) has developed the following further definition to the Four Stages of Adult Learning (see Figure 1 – non-italicised columns). Sims (2011, pp. 172–173) states that adding the theological perspective to the Four Stages of Adult Learning enables a theologically reflexive ministry, in that:

- in *sensing the presence and action of God*, the Clergyperson discerns where God is present and where God is acting. This requires humility and attentiveness;
- in *discerning God's purpose*, the Clergyperson is required to stand back from the situation and reflect on what may be God's desires for the person(s) with whom they are ministering, as

well as God's hopes for the way that they are
ministering;

- in *integrating into one's theology*, questions of
consistency with current practice of ministry or
faith, are asked. Holding the tensions within
personal theology may be required;

- and in *deciding to co-operate with God*, the
Clergyperson's personal theology may be
revised which leads to new implications for
pastoral and ministerial practice.

All of these aspects inform the person's current and future
practice. Sims (2011) states that if such reflective practice is
engaged with, then learning can be deep, and different from
much of the 'surface learning' that goes on in ordination
training. He concludes that 'quality' ministry is more likely
when theologically reflective practice is engaged in using
his proposed theological lens of "*sensing the presence and
action of God, discerning God's purpose, integrating into one's
theology,* and *deciding to co-operate with God*" (p. 175). Sims'
(2011) notion of theological reflective practice has much to
commend it, but to make it 'theologically *reflexive* practice',
Gubi (2019) has suggested another column focussed on
reflexivity: "What am I noticing about myself in relation to
other, and how might I 'be' different?" (see Figure 1 –
italicised column). This further level of awareness, required
of reflexivity, enables a deepening of the awareness of the
part (and the past) that the person brings to the encounter,
or to the experience, that the person is faced with. This, in
addition to the other areas of attention identified by Sims
(2011), arguably provides a more reflexive response, which
enhances self-awareness and deepens insight, enabling a

better pastoral and theological response, in keeping with the development of reflexive theology and reflective practice.

Kelly (2013) argues for a movement away from *habitus* (i.e. the acquisition of knowledge) to *phronesis* (i.e. practical wisdom which involves developing sound judgement and wisdom formed from reflection on previous experience to inform practice in the present). Kelly (2013) argues for *group* theological reflective practice, in which someone presents a *verbatim* (i.e. an experience that they have encountered). The facilitator encourages the other group participants to respond to what has been presented in a way that is non-judgemental and tentative, using three types of response that reflect types of Greek words used in the discovery of the empty tomb in John 20:1–9 – notice (*blepo*), wonder [or theorise (*theoreo*)], and realise (*horao*). In preparation, the presenter of the *verbatim* engages with the following questions (summarised from Kelly, 2013, p. 249):

- What was this experience about – for other(s) and for me?
- Whose need was being met – and how?
- What were its implications for other(s) and for me?
- What does it tell me about my pastoral ability?
- What questions does it raise about God, my values, beliefs, worldview/frame of reference?

Kelly (2013, pp. 250–252) found that 95% felt that the experience had impacted positively on their spiritual care practice (identified as: it encouraged a habit of continual reflection on practice and on developing self-awareness, it alerted participants to their own developing spiritual needs, it enhanced their spiritual lives, it enabled them to filter

Learning Strategy	Learning Environment	Primary Mode	Reflexive Perspective	Theological Perspective
Concrete Experience	Emphasising Personal Experiences	Feeling or Getting Involved	*Growing awareness of how I am feeling*	Sensing the Presence and Action of God
Reflective Observation	Understanding Concepts	Watching	*Awareness of what this is tapping into for me*	Discerning God's Purpose
Abstract Conceptualisation	Preferred Logical Thinking	Creating Ideas	*Making sense of how I am feeling and responding*	Integrating Into One's Theology
Active Experimentation	Applying Knowledge and Skills	Making Decisions and Doing	*Trying out a different way of being*	Deciding to Co-Operate with God

Figure 1. Adding *reflexivity* to Sims' (2011) Further Definition to the Four Stages of Adult Learning (Gubi, 2019)

content of what to share with patients); 85% felt that the experience of reflecting theologically together had positive effects on their relationships within their teams; 83% felt that the groups enhanced their resilience and vocational fulfilment (identified as a renewed sense of meaning and purpose in their spiritual care practice, and as a means of staying well in a demanding and draining role). These are impressive results. Kelly concludes his research article by translating what has been developed as group theological reflective practice, into what he terms 'Values Based Reflective Practice', in an attempt to promote its use as embedded practice within a secular healthcare service. In so doing, Kelly arguably gives more attention to the reflexive elements of the focus by examining 'values', in that he promotes the questions (summarised from Kelly, 2013, pp. 254-255):

- Whose need(s) were met during the encounter?
- What does this experience tell me about my caring ability?
- What does it tell me about me?
- What questions does it raise about my values (that inform my attitudes and behaviours)? i.e. With whom did the power lie? Whose voice(s) dominated or has/have most value: Whose voice(s) was/were not heard or undervalued?
- What future action will you take in relation to this encounter? i.e. For the well-being of the patient/carer/member of staff or others involved? For your own future practice? For your own well-being?

These important questions are arguably less promoted in his group theological reflective practice, but belong there, along with the theological, in developing greater reflexivity among participants.

Ladd (2014), writing as a person who is responsible for Ministry and Formation at a Church of England Theological Education Institution (TEI), argues for a more 'embodied approach' to ministerial development, in which the minister is enabled "to work hard to attend, and help people to attend, to the subjectivity of the other" (p. 359). This can lead to the valuing of the contribution of each person in the life of the Church, which Ladd (2014) argues reflects Paul's desire for a Christian Community (1 Corinthians 11:17–14:40) that *honours minority voices* and promotes the discipline of *community discernment*. In arguing for this, Ladd unwittingly seems to express the experience of what can occur in Reflective Practice Groups:

> There is a mystery to the other that is not to be violated or controlled but protected on a journey in which identity and mutual knowing is formed through relationship. This journey of inter-subjectivity involves an attentive effort that [can be] described as the movement from 'sensation' to 'perception'. 'Sensation' sees the other as an object. 'Perception' is a deliberate choice to listen and not just to look. It is a journey in which we refuse to allow the relationship to be reduced to a single subjectivity, refuse to appropriate the other, but allow her to be 'other' in embodied relationship. Furthermore, this journey of openness to the subjectivity of the other is one in which we must be prepared to guard that subjectivity in ourselves and in the other. The goal is not fusion, but rather a relationship between two subjects, the intention of which is to leave to the other his or her subjectivity. [This allows rooms for] a silence [or

> 'third space'] in which there is room for genuine attention to difference, to the history of each, not least to the party whose history has most consistently been unheard ... This practice involves the developing of boundaried listening; the creating of a third space in community – a truly hospitable space – where people learn to attend to each other's personhood. This challenges the temptation to fusion, the melting away of human boundaries in a quest for 'the answer' or 'our way of doing things' that preoccupies the life of so many communities, consciously or subconsciously. (Ladd, 2014, p. 359)

Ladd argues that theological reflection needs to be learned in context and in relationship (community), *as spiritual discernment*. Ladd then argues for a greater emphasis in theological education on learning in placement, supervised by 'educational practitioners' who are engaged in self-aware theological reflection on ministry. However, Ladd's arguments are a strong justification for the development of Reflective Practice Groups in TEIs, as a way of

> building reflective 'hubs' of (6–8) students ... that enable theological reflection in context to be the heart of ministerial training with genuine attention to what it takes to form community that attends to people's subjectivity, and which is at home in building relationship with the stranger ... and encourages reflective learning and development as a norm for ministers and congregations alike. (p. 363)

Using Reflective Practice Groups in ordination training

Whilst group work does often exist in ordination training, in my experience these groups often do not sufficiently fulfil the definition of Reflective Practice Groups as they are either too structured, contain a formal educative agenda, meet too infrequently or do not seem to give participants much time to explore anything at depth. All of these groups appear to be tutor-led, or tutor-facilitated, which potentially establishes a difficult dynamic within the participants of being able to express honest reflection, whilst knowing that they are being formally assessed (implicitly, if not explicitly), making the spaces potentially 'measured' in terms of what can be shared – "will they ordain me if I express my doubts of faith?" In counsellor training contexts, personal development groups (a form of Reflective Practice Group) are usually facilitated by external facilitators who have no assessment role, for this reason, thereby enabling a more honest and open reflection (Johns, 2012; Rose, 2008; Lennie, 2007). Whilst Reflective Practice Groups are not the only method of facilitating self-awareness and reflectivity (Nash and Nash, 2009), they enable core assumptions, beliefs, values and attitudes to be made visible to the person because of the group interaction. These colour our interactions and relationships with other people, our perceptions and feelings about the world and the meaning of life (Johns, 2012). Within a spiritual formation context, there is a need for a place where an ordinand can feel held and supported, as s/he moves from a more unquestioned acceptance of faith into a deeper mysticism of faith which is characterised by uncertainty, as reflexivity and faith develop. Reflective Practice Groups can provide a space where assumptions, beliefs, values and attitudes can be fully revealed and tested in comparison with others' attitudes, through gaining responses and feedback from other people, and from seeing and feeling how behaviour, which is driven by our values, directly affects and perceived by other members of our world (McLeod and McLeod, 2014; Johns, 2012; Rose, 2008; 2012).

Much has been written about the value and process of groups in the psychological literature (e.g. Preston-Shoot, 2007; Jaques and Salaman, 2006), and they are valued as a means of developing self-awareness (Johns, 2012; Mearns, 1997). Johns (2012, p. 157) states that being in a Reflective Practice Group can:

- [enable] experience in interactions with other people in very concrete and immediate ways, which can reinforce effective interpersonal patterns, challenge unhelpful ones and allow for possible changes to be tested out;
- reduce loneliness and isolation belonging to age and stage, life space or existential uncertainties by providing a supportive, bonded, at times loving, connection with peers in a shared, purposeful activity;
- provide opportunities to see and feel the consequences of our projections of others;
- offer, in other group members, a range of alternative models of being, behaving and communicating which may assist in us loosening or even changing some of our own constructs and straitjackets in feeling, thinking and acting.

Dryden, Horton, and Mearns (1995) regard the Reflective Practice Group as a vibrant context for identifying personal development needs. If an atmosphere of trust and spirit of encounter can be developed in a group, the members can help each other identify needs which might otherwise have been blind spots. Lennie (2007) points out that the participants of Reflective Practice Groups share relationships in other spheres which may impact on how an individual communicates within the group, and whether they get to know others in a meaningful way or remain hidden within the group. Within the American Catholic Church, Reflective Practice Groups are used in ordination training to cultivate spirituality (Foster et al., 2006) – their purpose is "the creation of a space in a busy calendar to tend to students' spiritual growth, and to centre the spiritual life of the seminary community thus contributing to the students' spiritual development" (p. 281).

Including Reflective Practice Groups in the curriculum
As the formation criteria for ordinands have moved towards developing a greater ability to be reflexive (The Archbishops' Council of the Church of England, 2003; Church of England, 2014), and towards lifelong learning in ministerial education (Ward, 2005), so the pedagogy within TEIs is changing to accommodate these formation requirements. This shift in pedagogy, with the use of Reflective Practice Groups, will enable 'deep learning' (Rhymes, 1993; Harkness, 2012).

In my experience of working in Higher Education Institutions, there is always a pressure to cover an extensive curriculum in a finite period of time, which is measured against learning outcomes. Ixer's (1999; 2010) main objection to reflective practice is that, in his view, reflectivity cannot be measured objectively – although a person's sense of their own growth and development (psychologically and theologically) can be expressed subjectively, with the inner journey and thinking demonstrated through journalling and written assignments (Bolton, 2014). Many TEIs run a mixed mode of attendance (full-time and part-time), with some being residential courses and some being non-residential. TEIs have had to develop a flexible approach to ordination training to accommodate an increase in those who are intending to serve in non-stipendiary ministry (or localised unpaid ministry) who also work full-time whilst training (Reiss, 2013). Therefore, the argument can be convincingly made, that to include a Reflective Practice Group on a regular basis, is to appear to have to accommodate another 'something' in an already tight schedule of material to cover. However, Reflective Practice Groups can enable a 'letting go' of some of the more formal approaches to learning through 'input' (surface learning), to enable a more informal, but boundaried, space to emerge in which learning can take place from within the group, following the group's agenda for learning (Where is my/ your dissonance or joy? What am I/you learning about my/ yourself in this experience? Where is God in this? How might I have done that better?), i.e. Ladd's (2014) 'embodied approach'.

The benefits of Reflexive Practice Groups in ordination training
The place of Reflective Practice Groups in supporting Clergy is increasingly researched and documented (e.g. Gubi, 2016; Gubi and Korris, 2015; Barrett, 2010; Travis, 2008). Gubi (2016) demonstrates that a Reflective Practice Group is a place where the seeds of self-reflection are sown and nurtured. These seeds can continue to be nurtured after training, as a culture of taking part in Reflective Practice Groups would have been established. The essential nature of developing self-awareness in building self-sufficiency and resilience, and the role of Reflective Practice Groups in assisting that development, is evident in the literature (Gubi and Korris, 2015; Barrett, 2010; Travis, 2008). Gubi (2016) identifies that Reflective Practice Groups can enable a better culture of self-care to be established, alongside the development of a more fluid attitude to ministry and

theology. The inclusion of Reflective Practice Groups in TEIs is beneficial in enabling ordinands to function with a kind of psychological literacy. Reflective Practice Groups can be a pedagogy that enables ordinands to flourish and feel more supported in their training and ministries. The benefits of Reflective Practice Groups are identified in the literature (Gubi, 2016; Gubi and Korris, 2015; Barrett, 2010; Travis, 2008) as offering support, enabling Clergy to feel less isolated, enabling Clergy to gain an insight into the way that they think and into the impact of their way of being on others. They enable Clergy to respect difference better and to gain a better sense of self-care. The Reflective Practice Group enables Clergy to engage in a better quality of pastoral encounter with others and to interact better with others in their ministry. It empowers Clergy to grow as human beings, enabling trust and vulnerability to be experienced safely. The Reflective Practice Group is identified as equipping Clergy to: negotiate boundaries better; feel listened to and valued; learn to listen to others better; learn from others; value one's own ministry more; have space to think and reflect; receive permission to be one's self; gain the realisation that one is not alone in the struggles of ministry; have a place to vent frustrations and express difficulties; and have a place to reflect theologically and practically (Gubi 2016). So, there is evidence that Reflective Practice Groups are effective in supporting Clergy in their ministry, and the culture of seeking support from Reflective Practice Groups can begin in TEIs.

Formulating practice
Charry (1997, p. 18) argues for forms of 'divine pedagogy' in TEIs, which are the means by which theology is developed. This development informs the processes which

enable the formation of character and assist in the building and maintaining of the community of faith. This formation and building enables the communication of that faith to the wider world. Kinast (1996, p. 20) states that there is a divine dimension to the origin of all experience which requires the ability to reformulate one's theology in order to express the truth which the theology intends (p. 122). This involves the use of reflexivity in the formation of ordinands. Denniston (2014) states that developing this level of reflexivity demands time to reflect honestly and a willingness to be vulnerable to re-enter a dissonant situation and consider the situation critically from a variety of perspectives. The reflexive element to this involves a search of self, and of one's own process, to know what one has brought to an experience (or encounter), as well as engaging with the perceptions of tradition, faith positions and biblical understanding, towards a personal and theological reflection, and an appropriate pastoral response. One place in which to develop this level of reflexivity and *phronesis* is Reflective Practice Groups.

As a means of formulating practice, Gubi (2019) advocates some 'foci for reflexivity'. These foci for reflexivity enable a fairly systematic approach for the development of reflexivity within the Reflective Practice Group context and include the psychological and the spiritual/theological. Recommendations for instigating Reflective Practice Groups are:

- That the Reflective Practice Group is not structured in its content (i.e. it is non-directive, but focussed on psychological and spiritual process, holding the foci for reflection in Figure 2 with attention). The content emerges from what is 'around' for the group participants.

- Reflective Practice Groups should consist of between six and 10 participants who negotiate an agreement (covenant or contract) consisting of confidentiality and practicalities (time, place, frequency, cost).

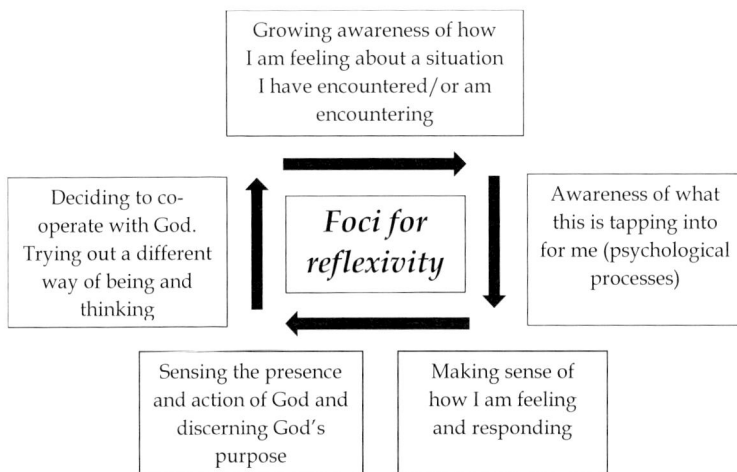

Figure 2. Foci for reflexivity in Reflective Practice Groups

- The Reflective Practice Group should meet weekly in Theological Colleges/Seminaries (preferably), and monthly in dioceses or Church communities, for at least one and a half hours (preferably two hours).
- The Reflective Practice Group should be facilitated by an external facilitator (who is preferably counsellor/ psychotherapy trained and not on the staff of the same Theological College/Seminary as the participants, or who is likely to have dual relationships with participants) who is trained in group facilitation and

group process, and who is able to facilitate at a spiritual- and psychological-process level.

- The facilitator keeps the group focussed on the internal reflexivity task, and the sharing within the group of that, embodying and exemplifying a quality of servanthood, service and hospitality. The time is not to be divided equally between participants, nor does everyone have to speak. However, a good facilitator will 'notice' and 'invite' non-contributors as appropriate.
- Participants, too, will be encouraged to listen deeply, share appropriately and facilitate each other with the foci for reflexivity in mind.
- Having two facilitators for each group has its own (arguably useful) dynamic, but given the limited financial resources in many communities, having two facilitators is not necessary.
- Facilitators hold awareness mindfully of the aspects that may limit a group and do what they can to overcome them where possible.
- Because there is always the potential for the process to become unhelpful, facilitators will need to be in supervision.
- Facilitators will also need to be able to facilitate fluidly in ways that move relatively easily between the spiritual (theological) and the psychological.

Conclusion

This Chapter has argued the value of Reflective Practice Groups in ordination training. Utilising Reflective Practice Groups in TEIs supports *formation*, develops *phronesis*, and enables the spiritual discernment and theological reflection that Ladd (2014) advocates, to be developed *in community*.

Chandler's (2009) research identifies Reflective Practice Groups as a valuable form of support. Chandler further identifies 'spiritual dryness' as a primary predictor of emotional exhaustion. Because of this, Chandler emphasises that "by virtue of their calling, [pastors] need to nurture an ongoing and renewing relationship with God, to maintain life balance, reduce stress and avoid burnout" (p. 284). Chandler concludes her research by arguing that "seminaries ... [i.e. TEIs] can assist their candidates to develop healthy personal practices [and should be] a crucial curricular consideration" (p. 285). With the emphasis within the 'Formation Criteria for Ordained Ministry' now on the development of reflectivity (Church of England, 2014, pp. 10–15), Reflective Practice Groups would be a helpful way of responding to those formation criteria, developing a heart theology, and fostering good self-care practices for future ministry. But what might the limitations of Reflective Practice Groups be?

CHAPTER SIX:

THE LIMITATIONS OF REFLECTIVE PRACTICE GROUPS

Peter Madsen Gubi

Introduction

Reflective Practice Groups give opportunity for openness and honesty before others, and members are required to work towards finding a way to both hold vulnerability and affirm the confidence and authority of the other. They provide a chance for participants to tell their story, to give and receive support and encouragement in the situation in which each incumbent finds him/herself, and that can be taken back into the life and ministry of each member.

However, they do not suit everyone (Miles and Proeschold-Bell, 2013) and they do have their limitations. Williams and Irving (1996) suggest that Reflective Practice-type groups only sometimes lead to positive outcomes. They can sometimes be destructive (Lieberman, 1983) and dysfunctional (Lennie, 2007). Benson (1987) observes the 'negatives' of Reflective Practice Groups as: feeling excluded or scapegoated; suffering the insensitivities, righteous, relevant or inappropriate anger and clumsiness of others; feeling unsafe and uncontained, over-dependent on or hostile to peers or group leaders; feeling bored, frustrated, impotent or critical of self and/or others – all of which can occur for group participants at any time. Moon (2004) states that not all people find reflexivity easy, and Robson and Robson (2009) argue that such groups do not always feel 'safe'. Gubi and Korris' (2015) participants identified other participants sometimes giving answers and sometimes not listening as a limitation.

The Limitations of Reflective Practice Groups

In 2017 and 2019, Peter conducted some research (Gubi, 2017; Gubi, 2020) into the limitations of Reflective Practice Groups to attempt to establish what kinds of issues hindered the experience of a Reflective Practice Group. This Chapter is based on the findings of those two pieces of research.

What the research says about the limitations of Reflective Practice Groups

In Gubi (2017), the research question that focussed this research was, "do Reflexive Groups have a beneficial place in Clergy training, and in supporting Clergy, towards enabling a more effective ministry?" The aim was to discover if, and how, Reflective Practice Groups support Clergy, and what might limit their effectiveness (the focus of this Chapter). The research was conducted in two stages using a mixed methods approach. In Stage One, 42 Bishop's Advisors for Pastoral Care and Counselling were emailed to ascertain how many of them facilitated Reflective Practice Groups, or knew of such groups in their dioceses, and to ask if they could be interviewed if they did. These Bishop's Advisors have responsibility for advising on the provision of mental health care and well-being for the Clergy in their dioceses. Eight Bishop's Advisors (a response rate of 19%) responded to indicate that they facilitate (or have facilitated) Reflective Practice Groups in their dioceses. They were sent a participant information sheet explaining the details of the research. Semi-structured interviews were set up with the eight respondents. These were digitally audio-recorded and transcribed, and based on the following questions:

- Can you tell me something about the reflexive-type group(s) that you facilitate, or that run in your diocese?

- What might limit or hinder the group(s)?

The data were analysed using a thematic analysis (Braun et al. , 2015). Data attributed to Bishop's Advisors were coded with 'BA' and a number (e.g. BA2) to protect anonymity. In Stage Two, an online survey, using the research instrument 'Bristol Online Survey', was sent to 64 Reflective Practice Group participants, identified by the Bishop's Advisors of three dioceses, with the permission of each diocese. The online survey was sent by blind-copied email from each diocesan office (to preserve the anonymity of the participants, as the diocesan offices already knew who the participants were). The questions in the online survey were based on the data from the Bishop's Advisors' interviews, and asked participants to agree or disagree with the following statements:

I have found that my involvement with my Reflective Practice Group has been held back by:

- my difficulty in committing the time to attend regularly
- my difficulty in sharing openly with others
- my difficulty in making time to prioritise attendance
- others in the group
- the manner of facilitation
- the structured nature of the sessions
- the unstructured nature of the sessions
- the cost
- feeling unsafe

The purpose of the statements was to discover if the Reflective Practice Groups' participants experienced the same limitations as the claims that the Bishop's Advisors were making about the limiting factors of the groups. The data attributable to each diocese is coded with a D (for diocese) and a number (1, 2 or 3). Within Diocese 1, the online survey was sent to 29 participants. This process was repeated across all three dioceses. Sixteen participants responded in D1 (response rate 55.2%). Within D2, the survey was sent to eight participants. Seven participants responded (response rate 87.5%). In D3, the survey was sent to 27 participants. Fourteen participants (P) responded (response rate 51.8%).

Stage one findings

The data from the Bishop's Advisors are presented under the following headings:

- Time
- Scary
- Needs are too big
- Boundaries
- Prayer
- Lacking commitment
- Being sent
- Poor facilitation
- Not for everyone
- Struggles with expectation

Time

All of the BAs felt that the inability of Clergy to commit the time was a hindrance factor. BA5 described it in this way:

I think that's why a lot of clergy don't take this up because they – I mean for four years we ran eighteen sessions a year. This year, I've done fourteen sessions just to make it slightly less time intensive as I thought that was an issue for people. For some clergy, even the thought of meeting with their colleagues in that kind of setting, fortnightly, I think just might have felt too much. (BA5)

However, BA3 felt that the Church needed to address this culture of busyness to prioritise time for the development of self-awareness:

Cultural busyness needs to be attacked, because people will say they are too busy, there are too many other things to do, but actually if the church really, really recognises that self-awareness is fundamental to the efficacy of somebody in ministry, then it's a priority, and there should be time. (BA3)

Scary
Engaging 'at depth' is not something that many Clergy do and is therefore scary.

I think the cost of opening up to a whole load of people, on that kind of regular basis, is scary for people. (BA5)

Needs are too big
Sometimes, people left the group because their needs were too much, either for the participant, or the group, to handle. BA5 stated that,

The two people who, over the five years I've been doing the group, have left. It has become clear that their needs were too big for the group. In both cases, they just couldn't somehow use the group. Their needs have just been utterly overwhelming and somehow they couldn't bear the group and the sharing or something. They'd get very frustrated and angry within the group where you felt there was a different agenda somehow, something going on. I think unconsciously they might have had unreal expectations of the group actually, so they had to find a way to leave it and, in the end, I think that was probably better that that happened. (BA5)

There is an indication here that Reflective Practice Groups may not be for everyone in that psychological or relational damage may exacerbate difficulties for the groups and for the individuals.

Boundaries

Careful selection of candidates for each group emerged as a theme, as dual boundaries may act as a hindrance to full use of the group experience:

> *If I felt there was going to be a boundary clash of people who were working too much together already outside, I'd address that and talk about it, but I'd probably not put them in the same group together.* (BA5)

BA4 stated that many of her group participants travel some distance to what might be thought of as a 'neutral' space, so as to avoid dual-boundaries.

> *Yes, they generally all travel to it and appreciate being outside their deanery in what is a neutral space for all of them, completely neutral, but it is a space away from their parishes and they specifically wanted that.* (BA4)

BA3 had actual experience of not taking into better consideration the mix of the group and their potential dual boundaries:

> *Also, the fact that there was only one woman and four men. Three of the men came from the same deanery which was a very male dominated deanery, so the deanery-chapter competitiveness remained. So, the showing of vulnerability was the last thing they wanted to do because they were like that any way, and so the last thing they wanted to do was to be engaged in doing this in public.* (BA3)

The consequences of these dual relationships were:

> *Any question of looking more deeply at what might be going on, and what internal drivers there might be, or of helping others to explore where they might be, that wasn't what they wanted so they tended to be full of – if we ever got anywhere near something significant, then they would change the subject, get full of anecdotes, problem solved, anything.* (BA3)

However, BA3 realised that it was not always possible to be mindful of dual boundaries:

> *To be put in a group where there is somebody with whom there is antipathy and which could lead to bullying or stifling of your own stuff and it won't be addressed, that would be destructive. So, I do think it's better to have some element of choice in this but often, of course, that's not possible. It would depend on geography as to who you were with. I was facilitating last night, and somebody said, "well, I've got no choice because I can't travel. So, I have to be with people near me, but there is one person that I know I just don't want to talk to". So, I'm not sure it's going to be very helpful for her, but it might be.* (BA3)

BA6 also took care in the make-up of the groups:

> *So, we do look at it in terms of are there any obvious personality issues or previous divisions in this cohort? Are there any Churchmanship issues, like we don't want the most "forward in faith" one in with our most radical feminist theological lesbian, for example, ideally. So, we do gerrymander the group ... We would try and not have one woman and five men. We would try, perhaps to have two women in the group ... So we take some care with that and also whether there are connections with the facilitators, because sometimes there are, you know equally, you want to – you probably know there is too much of a dual relationship.* (BA6)

Prayer

Perhaps unexpectedly (given the Clergy context), three of the BAs felt that prayer did not have a place in Reflective Practice Groups as it could be a hindrance factor. BA5 stated:

> I just don't feel that the purpose of the group is to have prayer and wouldn't feel that that was appropriate. It is interesting that sometimes, at the end of a group, you often find a bit of an unconscious theme running through the group and you find that although ostensibly different, that the two presentations actually have thrown up similar themes and at the end of a group, one of us might make a sort of bit of a gathering comment and if it has been a particularly emotionally charged group, there is often just a little moment of silence which sort of happens naturally and I think that is just a sort of an awareness of something being shared and that is enough, yes … I suspect it puts off some of our more closed evangelical brothers and sisters. I think the open ones would be okay, but I think that you know, they would sort of, "why can't this happen?" sort of thing … It's part of their church culture, but on the other hand, having a different start to a meeting which usually begins and ends in prayer, is also helpful. (BA5)

For BA4, the experience was similar, except that it was the group that requested that they do not pray, because every Church group begins and ends with prayer, and it was important to the group that this group was different:

> One of the things we talked about in the beginning was about where the group members might come from … theologically their needs are in different places. It's about respecting difference. And we talked about the place of prayer in the group and what they wanted to do about that, and they all said they would not want to start with prayer. Because that sort of becomes an expectation – and every meeting starts with prayer and so it was agreed that, and not only that but then it's "who's turn is it now"? And I just want to come here and I

123

just want to be and I don't want to think, "oh, I've got to do the prayers today". (BA4)

BA8 also highlighted the impact that prayer can have on what has been shared:

> *... prayer, and that is a really interesting one because my sense of that is where group members in the early starting off of the group, very occasionally, actually surprisingly, have said, "do we start with prayer or can we end with a prayer?" and of course, I would always say, absolutely, we will now be silent for five minutes. Is it helpful or not, particularly at the end? And a new colleague came to supervision in the early stages and said it was awful because right at the end so-and-so bobbed up and basically disabled the whole of the material of the group by putting it into prayer. So I think, it is really important to be prayerful about the group and I hope they are before they come in, or that we can certainly end with silence and bring those things to God – but actually words are not necessarily the valuable part, and some clergy have found it very difficult.* (BA8)

Rather than this being about the use or non-use of prayer, per se, the importance here is in keeping reflective groups 'different' from other groups that Clergy are used to being in. As prayer marks the beginning and end of much group activity that the Clergy engage in, the non-use of prayer is a way of making the space 'different'. Prayer can also negate (spiritualise away) what has been shared in the group.

Lacking commitment

BA4 felt that the inability to commit to the process could hinder the benefits of Reflective Practice Groups:

> *Lack of commitment ... committing to the time, committing to attending ... making the time. Yes, and I think that's one of the reasons may be that they don't because how can I spare the*

time to come? – especially if they are coming a long way. Geographically, there's an hour to get there and then ..., so essentially they are giving up a morning, making the time in the diary for that is certainly a factor and one person recently commented on that, you know, newly first-time incumbent, "I don't think I've time for this. I've had to hit the ground running", and actually somebody said, "this is exactly why you do need to come". And she said, "actually yes, you are right". So, making that time ... prioritising ..., and that goes back to that thing if self-care is considered to be something essential then, prioritise it. So that's one thing both committing to time, committing to the process and you've got to feel safe. (BA4)

Commitment, here, is not just about time, but also about a willingness to engage in the process. BA7 also stressed that commitment was important, and that Clergy were poor at committing themselves to something that was for themselves:

Clergy are terrible with time, starting and ending. But you know, if they are committed to these groups, it comes before anything else – funerals, or the bishop wanting to see you. So you have that interplay, "Oh, I've got a funeral!" "Well, you did make a commitment." So you are having to educate them afresh about what does it mean to be committed and to put that first ... I think that is essential, and you are also helping them to realise that this is not a day off. Some of them will go, "oh, it's my day off!" This is work. (BA7)

Being sent

Being 'sent' was identified as a hindering factor:

They were sent and they found it quite difficult to engage with the group process. There was always a funeral or something else that meant that unfortunately they were unable to come, so we never got, only twice I think in a year, the cohorts, all cohort of five and they were very defensive and things were very 'out-there' and it was hard work. (BA3)

BA3 mentioned that some people were there simply to comply:

> *I think it is because they were the sort of people who did what the Bishop said, because that's what you do, but you don't go any further. You are there and that's it, so ... Any question of looking more deeply at what might be going on, and what internal drivers there might be, or of helping others to explore where they might be, that wasn't what they wanted. So, they tended to be full of bullshit!* (BA3)

The importance of this being a voluntary activity is highlighted.

Poor facilitation

BA3 mentioned the need to have good facilitation:

> *If you can't find the money to facilitate well, that's not going to be helpful. If you don't have a facilitator, you run the risk of it becoming a collusive, or moan, shop, but that doesn't mean it's not a good idea; it just means that it's not a panacea and it's got to be very carefully constructed and reviewed really ... When you've got the right facilitator, that can be identified, looked at, challenged, but if there is nobody there to make those connections, and those connections are not made, then they haven't learned very much, have they really? ... except that they hate groups.* (BA3)

Good external facilitation seems important in keeping the group engaged in process.

Not for everyone

BA3 felt that it was important to recognise that Reflective Practice Groups were not for everyone:

We set up a group for new incumbents because they were a group of people with stuff in common and often feel isolated and without support. It was a good idea to have a group. It wasn't compulsory. It was just there – an invitation, and one chap came and talked to me about this, and was incandescent with rage that he should be expected to waste time doing this when life was so busy. Why would he need a group? He already – he'd been dealing with stuff for a long time, so there was nothing he needed to know about things. I said, "I don't think it's that sort of group. I don't think it's to do with getting to know XXX. I think it's to do with them supporting each other and reflecting on practice". "Well, I can't be bothered with that sort of rubbish …" and there are always going to be people like that, and they are often the ones that undermine the efficacy of the group. So, in a sense, it would be good to find something else for them. But on the other hand, they may just learn something but one doesn't want them to wreck it for everybody else. I think you need a mixed economy. I think so much depends on really good facilitators and the right combination of people. (BA3)

Struggles with expectation

BA6 felt that part of the cultural struggle of participation involved the difference in expectation required of group participants:

It gets caught up in a bigger picture of authority. It seems to me to be something about the nature of the Church, that whenever they think the kind of "Bishop Daddy" wants you to do it, it becomes, "Oh ah THEY are making me", or "THEY think I should do this". Or, if you are an ordinand, it is likely to be, "IF I don't do this, THEY won't ordain me. (BA6)

There can sometimes be a clash of values espoused within the body-politic of the Church of England which can prevent Clergy from being able to engage with vulnerability.

Stage two findings

The statistical data from the Reflective Practice Groups' participants are presented in Table 2. The qualitative data from the Reflective Practice Groups' participants (Table 3. opposite) highlighted hindrance factors as: dual boundaries; the commitment of others in the group; the sometimes unhelpful/helpful structure/non-structure of the sessions; where a participant is in themselves; how the group 'fits' with other support structures that a participant has around them; and wanting prayer and blessing which may be perceived as manipulative. The cost was prohibitive for one participant.

Table 2. Collated statistical data from the online surveys of Dioceses 1, 2 and 3

No.	Statement: I have found that my involvement with my Reflective Practice Group has been held back by:	Diocese 1 Agree		Diocese 1 Disagree		Diocese 2 Agree		Diocese 2 Disagree		Diocese 3 Agree		Diocese 3 Disagree	
		%	n=	%	n=	%	n=	%	n=	%	n=	%	n=
1.	My difficulty in committing the time to attend regularly	12.5	2	87.5	14	0	0	100	7	7.1	1	92.9	13
2.	My difficulty in sharing openly with others	12.5	2	87.5	14	14.3	1	85.7	6	0	0	100	14
3.	My difficulty in making time to prioritise attendance	12.5	2	87.5	14	0	0	100	7	7.1	1	92.9	13
4.	Others in the group	0	0	100	16	28.6	2	71.4	5	7.1	1	92.9	13
5.	The manner of facilitation	12.5	2	87.5	14	0	0	100	7	0	0	100	14
6.	The structured nature of the sessions	6.7	1	93.3	14	0	0	100	7	0	0	100	14
7.	The unstructured nature of the sessions	6.7	1	93.3	14	0	0	100	7	0	0	100	14
8.	The cost	0	0	100	16	0	0	100	7	0	0	100	13
9.	Feeling unsafe	0	0	100	15	0	0	100	7	0	0	100	14
10.	Is there anything else that you would like to add about what hinders the group?												

Table 3. Participants' qualitative perspectives on the hindrance factors of Reflective Practice Groups

Response	Code
There is a conflict between the group and the diocesan structures. While it may work for those with only local roles, there can be a challenge where some have roles (themselves or within their families) across the diocese, which may intersect with the local roles.	D1P7
With regards to the structure, I have experienced two groups and the one in which there was a clearer structure of sharing, listening, contributing questions in turn was more beneficial. The facilitator in this group was simply that – and helped us to explore our own responses instead of offering too many responses of her own.	D1P1
None. It is one of my priorities.	D1P3
I have been very 'talked out' at times, as I was also receiving spiritual direction as well as individual counselling for managing depression.	D1P6
Sometimes it has felt a bit awkward knowing the others' spouses and remembering what was said where. Sometimes people wanting to 'pray' or asking for a blessing which feels manipulative rather than positive.	D2P2
Commitment of others in the group.	D3P5
How I am on the day.	D3P7
The cost.	D3P8

The hindrance factors to Reflective Practice Groups were stated by the BAs as:

- the inability of Clergy to prioritise and commit to the time;

- it was scary for participants to open up to their vulnerability with others;
- sometimes the needs of some of the participants were too big, and could sabotage the group;
- dual relationships with other group participants could cause complexity and hinder sharing;
- prayer;
- being sent by a Bishop or Archdeacon;
- the open agenda and style of facilitation does not suit some people;
- sometimes there are struggles with expectations because the Reflective Practice Group is culturally different from other groups found in the Church of England;
- and geographically, the distance of the Reflective Practice Group was prohibitive for some, although having to travel provided another reflective space for others.

However, these limitations were not the lived experience of the Reflective Practice Groups' participants (albeit they are self-selected participants who may have been predisposed not to have some of these problems), with only:

- 12.5% (D1), 0% (D2) and 7.1% (D3) finding it difficult to commit to the time;
- 12.5% (D1), 14.3% (D2) and 0% (D3) struggling to share openly with others;
- 0% (D1), 28.6% (D2) and 7.1% (D3) struggling with others in the group;
- 12.5% (D1) and 0% (D2 and D3) struggling with the style of facilitation;
- and with 0% (D1, D2 and D3) feeling unsafe.

Other hindering factors expressed in the qualitative data from the Reflective Practice Groups' participants included other external factors that were 'around' for participants (e.g., D1P6 expressed feeling over-supported because of the counselling and spiritual direction that s/he was also having), and the difficulties with dual boundaries (D1P7, D2P2). Whilst the concerns and experiences of the BAs are important things to be mindful of, and echo to some extent, Miles and Proeschold-Bell's (2013) research, the overwhelming evidence from the Reflective Practice Groups' participants in this research is that Reflective Practice Groups are more beneficial than not (i.e. the limitations were minimal for the Reflective Practice Groups' participants). The limitations are something to be mindful of, but are not prohibitive. Interestingly, given the context of the Reflective Practice Groups (i.e. for Clergy), prayer was considered by some (e.g., BA5, BA4 and BA8) to potentially hinder the group process or to spiritualise away the difficulties faced within the group. The lack of prayer also enabled the group to be established as 'different' from other Clergy groups and meetings (e.g. chapter meetings), which usually begin and end with prayer. Whilst these possibilities are things to be mindful of (Gubi, 2009), arguably the literature (e.g. Gubi, 2008) suggests that prayer can also add to a person's sense of well-being, and given that Chandler's (2009) research identifies 'spiritual dryness' as a primary predictor of emotional exhaustion in Clergy, prohibiting prayer seems counter-intuitive to the purpose of the group in promoting Clergy well-being. However, one of the Reflective Practice Group participants identified prayer as a hindrance to the group: "... *sometimes people wanting to 'pray', or asking for a blessing, which feels manipulative rather than positive* ..." (D2P2). So, it seems that mindfulness of these tensions is important, without losing sight of the importance of the spiritual.

Hindrance factors identified in an impact case study
In Gubi, (2020), two focus groups (G1 and G2) of Reflective Practice Group participants in a Church in Wales diocese were interviewed. The hindrances were identified as:

Suspicion
Both members of G1 expressed feeling profoundly sceptical and suspicious at the start of the group because they hadn't been given any clear sense of the structure or purpose of the group. There was a sense of this being "part of some sort of Big Brother deal from the diocese". One member of G1 expressed that it:

> took a lot to think through committing myself to the process, although I very much wanted to as I was extremely keen to be in reflective practice. (G1)

No choice
One participant in G1 expressed having been given no choice about the group to which they were allocated. It was allocated centrally.

Trust
Building trust at the start seemed important to all participants in both G1 and G2:

> "We began to realise that that fourth person would not fit in with the group, because there's a lot of trust involved in this group. It was about saying … you couldn't guarantee that what you said would remain confidential, whereas with the group we ended up with,

we knew we were alright. So, as we began to realise that, then the group began to work." (G1)

"We can trust confidentiality here, can't we? Because we all know each other but if you've got five or six different people who don't really know each other ... there's that trust." (G2)

The third member of G1 could not build the trust and left.

One-upmanship

One of the aspects that was identified as being potentially hindering of the process, was if the group became competitive, i.e. about one-upmanship. Neither group felt that that was present among their group. Comparing the experience of their Reflective Practice Group with another group that s/he had been in:

The feedback that I got from colleagues was that there was a sense of one-upmanship going on in the group. So, it was a question of, "'Well, I'm doing this in my parish. Aren't I marvellous?" and they weren't engaging with one another. They were being more competitive than complementary ... a phrase I once heard, I quite like, bitching or boasting, rather than sharing and supporting which is a problem. (G1)

Diocesan dynamics

For G1, the absence of having a diocesan Bishop at the time of the research had clearly impacted on what they brought to the group. They used it as an opportunity to reflect on their frustration as decisions weren't being made at diocesan level, which impacted significantly on them.

I must admit that what has happened in the diocese has overshadowed it so much, and, in a sense, I don't really feel we've had a year of reflecting on ministry practice. (G1)

However, for the participants in G2, the same difficulties were around, but were less intrusive to their experience of the group.

In our day-to-day work there is no doubt that the issue of what's been happening in the diocese and the Bishop and whatever that's been about and all the rest of that, there is no doubt that for all of us that's been a pain in the backside and it's made life very difficult. We've expressed those difficulties in this group, but I don't think it's been a hindrance in terms of how these groups have worked. (G2)

Uncertainty of the group

One aspect of hindrance that both groups mentioned, was the high dropout rate, which impacted on the experience of the group.

"The uncertainty about the makeup of the group is difficult, and then the group changing was difficult as well." (G1)

"We started with about six or seven of us and we've dwindled down to just the three of us now. And I found that a sadness when people have chosen to opt out. Now, I know why one person has opted out and I understand that and I'm happy with that but there's one person who's just not come. Came the first time and not seen them since and I find that odd. So, there's no explanation and there's not attendance so I find that more of a problem than competition." (G2)

"I was also a bit disappointed that people dropped out very close to the beginning and at that point I did wonder if we were going to survive. But apart from that I wouldn't say I've felt hindered." (G2)

There was a sense of a missed opportunity for G2 that younger members of the Clergy seemed less committed and hadn't felt that they could have benefitted from the experience and wisdom of the more experienced members of the group:

In just us three there's a wealth of experience and, I would like to add, wisdom that I think a younger person could tap into. By opting not to be part of this group then you don't have the opportunity of tapping into that joint and massive experience. (G2)

Having benefitted from the group, there was a lack of empathy with those who dropped out:

I have been surprised that I've not resented coming. I've not got up and thought, "Oh, I could really do without this today." I've thought, "I'm going up to XXX. XXX'll be there and it'll be fine." (G2)

Conclusion

The participants felt that the following might be hindering factors (for some): the uncertain dynamics within the particular diocese (in that they didn't have a Bishop at the time of the groups and decisions weren't being made which caused immense frustration for some); a sense of suspicion (for some) around the motives of the diocese for hosting Reflective Practice Groups (i.e. is this 'Big Brother' at work?); not being given a choice of which group to belong to; a lack of trust that some seemed unable to gain (and who then left); a sense of competitiveness in the group; and by the uncertainty of the viability of the group when others left.

Reflective Practice Groups are not the panacea for providing Clergy support – they are one form of support. It seems that careful planning to avoid dual boundaries is imperative, as is the provision of good external facilitators who are not part of diocesan dynamics. This will have a financial impact. Voluntary participation is essential, as this enhances commitment and minimises sabotage of the process. It seems important to emphasise the importance of commitment when embarking on participation in Reflective Practice Groups. Those who struggle relationally, or whose psychological damage may be exacerbated by the experience, arguably may need a different form of support (e.g. personal counselling). Attendance at Reflective Practice Groups should not be expected, but rather, encouraged. Carefully facilitating a reduction in uncertainty, suspicion and competitiveness if any of these traits are present, should occur. Given the perceived benefits of Reflective Practice Groups (Barrett, 2010; Gubi, 2016; Gubi and Korris, 2015; Travis, 2008), the limitations should not be seen as prohibitive for everyone, but something to hold in mind when assessing the provision of such support.

CHAPTER SEVEN:

REFLECTIONS ON FACILITATING
A REFLECTIVE PRACTICE GROUP

William West

Introduction

A few years ago, I facilitated a Reflective Practice Group for some Clergy in the north of England. In this Chapter, I intend to reflect on my experiences of being in, and with, this group. I will draw on my notes (which I made immediately after each group), my end of group report, and other notes I have made subsequently. I will not be dwelling on group members' individual experiences, or personal details, as this would break confidentiality. I will focus on my own experiences, on some general experiences common to group members, and on my final reflections about the value of such groups, and where they might well fit alongside other support for best practice by Clergy.

I have considerable experience of facilitating groups for counselling and psychotherapy, including personal development groups and supervision groups for trainee counsellors. In addition, I have several friends, colleagues and ex-students who are ordained. This, however, was my first experience of facilitating a Reflective Practice Group for ordained ministers. So, my comments need to be seen in this light.

This group met every month, for a couple of hours, for nearly two years, and group members were able to reflect on their work. It had a huge impact on me including challenging my assumptions about ministers, some of which were buried quite deeply in me. I am not myself ordained, although my evolving religious faith is very important to me. It was, therefore, curious to be facilitating a group whose members shared a role that I had never experienced. This contrasts with my experience of group and individual supervision of therapists and trainee therapists, as I have been a trainee therapist and am now an experienced therapist and Counsellor trainer. Also, in such groups, for example, we usually share the same ethical code, and notions about being (or rather, not being) fit to practice.

The group experience

As I have already stated, it does not feel appropriate for me to write in particular detail about any one participant and what they brought to the group. However, some general comments are worth making. The group members did seem to get the idea of the group as a place in which they could reflect on their working lives (and home lives where relevant) fairly quickly, and the challenges they faced in their work. In that sense, the group members made good use of the group. I responded verbally and non-verbally to this sharing, sometimes drawing their attention to possible practical ways forward or responding therapeutically to what they shared. Over time, group members also became more willing and able to respond to one another in similar ways.

I decided to begin and end the group sessions with a time of quiet reflection. After a few sessions, one member of the group asked if we could begin and close the group with prayer. I was initially troubled by this notion and wondered if this participant was challenging my leadership of the group. However, on reflection and consideration in my own supervision, it became clear to me that this was well worth exploring. The suggestion met with group members' approval so, each time we met, I invited whoever was willing to begin and end the session with a prayer. What followed were some appropriate and very effective examples of spontaneous prayer. Although this initially took me out of my therapeutic comfort zone, it appealed to the religious side of my nature. It is interesting that I did not feel able to offer any prayers myself, but I was in the company of experts in prayer!

Various other insights emerged for me over the course of this group. I found myself developing deep admiration and respect for the ministers involved – especially their 'on call' status which was even more intensive if they lived near to their Church, or even in the vicarage. I also noticed the disappearance of the traditional role of the Clergy wife. These days many Clergy partners have their own careers and the more recent role of the Clergy husband does not carry the same expectations as the (traditional) Clergy wife does. However, ministers remain central figures for their congregations. The women Clergy in the group were clearly under differing stresses and expectations from their congregations, as were the men, and they were often also wives and mothers.

I was touched by the faith of the Clergy members in my group which was, at times, expressed within the group, and this had a deep impact on my own religious journey at that time. Some of the life challenges they faced echoed those of mine – either current or previous – to a greater or lesser extent. It was clear that their faith had not made them perfect, nor had it insulated them from suffering.

My own experience of the group
It seems useful to explore the impact of the group on me – both as an example of the challenges of this work, but also to show the issues that remained with me after each session.

This was then explored by me in my own supervision, to guide my work with the group. I will use some direct quotes (in italics) taken from my notes immediately following each session of the group. People soon began sharing about the challenges of their work and I felt an admiration for their work and began to wonder about my usefulness to them.

After a few sessions, I found myself writing "*Things went well today with a focus on their role(s) and responsibilities and not taking things too personally.*" I found it useful, especially in the run up to the busy time of Christmas, to introduce the notion of 'fitness to practice' which was well-engaged with – "*General sharing about how they looked after themselves after a prompt from me about 'fitness to practice.'*" A few months later, I found myself writing, "*I had a sense of the impossibility of their jobs and how they had to decide what they could do, when.*" It became clear that some of their work was especially challenging, including opening their Churches to offer lunches and food banks, and "*I was very touched by three of them talking about working with asylum seekers, including court cases.*"

It seemed a feature of my own counter-transference[7] with this group, to question my own usefulness to them – "*I felt humble as if I had not done much but hold the ring – deep sharing occurred though.*" This reminds me of a recent supervisee I had, who worked in schools with often very troubled children, and I found myself feeling not very helpful with him. Eventually, it occurred to me that maybe this was what my supervisee was feeling! So, perhaps, at

---

[7] "It has become widely accepted that the emotional response of the therapist to the client, the 'counter-transference', is an essential source of data about what is happening in the therapy" (McLeod, 2009, p. 99).

some deep and maybe even unconscious level, some of the group members questioned the value of what they were doing. *"It felt like hard work listening to their stories and stress."* It was a challenge to be present and listen to them without having any easy answers – but again, is this a reflection of their experience as ministers?

"X talked about filling in a form about how many hours he worked and his realisation that it was not sustainable long term." This was a real trigger to them thinking out loud about how they manage their time – when they are 'on call', but also when they allow themselves not to be available. *"A lot of talk in the group today about the value of physical exercise."* One apparently useful response to stress was a focus on physical activity. Whether they could deliver on their suggestions about this is perhaps another matter. This led subsequently to *"some focus on their skills set and spiritual discipline so they would be 'fit for practice'"*. At a later session, one of the group members provides a list of Clergy roles. *"Y's list of clergy roles provoked some deep reflection on their roles and what their responsibilities are, and how 'perfect' they need to be. Their challenge was to not overwork in a not smart way."*

It is always interesting to see how one feels when a group like this comes to its final session. *"Final meeting of the group, I felt sad walking into the meeting place which took me by surprise. I had been touched by working with them and would miss them."* There was also a sense of relief; the group had been a challenge for me to facilitate, to come up against what their work asked of them and how it impacted on them, not always in a healthy way.

Supervision
It was very helpful having regular supervision of my work with the Reflective Practice Group to enable me to do my

best possible facilitation. I found it useful to arrange my supervision sessions to occur where possible within a couple of days of the group meeting. This meant that my memory and experience of the group was still very fresh and vivid.

It was something of a challenge for me to make sense of the ministers' world, of their work and to not merely see everything through a counselling/psychotherapy lens. Despite my own keen interest in the relationship between religion, spirituality and therapy, it was also curious to be facilitating this group during a time of religious change for me as I found a new religious home shortly before the group commenced. So, my own faith was particularly alive to me at that time. Supervision helped me stay as clear as possible and kept me focussed on the task at hand. It was most useful that I had a long-established supervisory relation with my supervisor that preceded the Reflective Practice Group, and which continues to this day.

Clergy stress

> The poor psychological health of some clergy is well-documented in the literature. It is often brought about by poor boundaries, inadequate self-care, emotional isolation, a lack of privacy for clergy families, and many pulls on clergies' time. (Gubi, 2016, p. 2)

Over the almost two years of the group, I was struck by the levels of stress involved in the lives of my participants. This was not only stress caused by the varying and unpredictable demands of the job but also, in a number of instances, from events involving family members. Three members of the group had children still at school. I was struck by the fact that the stresses involved impacted differently on the women than on the men in the group. This is too small a sample to draw any definitive conclusions from, but I suspect that congregations have differing, if overlapping, expectations on women Clergy as opposed to men, and that women still probably do more family and domestic duty than men. I am not at all sure that the Clergy husbands play the same part as the Clergy wives.

With regard to this stress, I did feel as if the Clergy in my group were/are rather like GPs, in that the next phone call or person at the door could be either someone with a simple demand for time and attention, or equally someone with literally a life and death situation. So, that sense of being 'on call', and how to handle it, was very present, especially for those living in a vicarage attached to a Church. I noticed that one participant regularly took an overnight stay away from home to handle stress levels.

Francis (2018) has researched and written extensively about Clergy stress, and maintains that the causes of Clergy burnout are due to their personal management of their ministry rather than to external factors. However, it is apparent that Clergy's own personal management of their work is inevitably influenced by their training and line management. Francis (2018) also insists that, from a review of Clergy work-related psychological health, psychological factors provide the strongest prediction of Clergy well-being. This suggests that psychologically helping Clergy, in ordination training and afterwards, to effectively handle the challenges of their work, is crucial. However, it is important that we do not blame Clergy for how they handle stress; severe stress has a negative impact on people regardless of their psychology.

Gubi and Korris (2015) summarise the research into the poor psychological well-being of Clergy as follows:

Clergy often offer a 24-hour service to those in need. Their homes are a point of contact for the homeless and those with mental health issues and addictions. Clergy families are often in the community spotlight in a way that other families are not. Clergy tend to be introvert, so the more social expectations of the work can be challenging. Often, they are faced with unrealistic projections/expectations from others, which can create significant difficulties if they go unrecognised and, even in the self-aware, the painful experience of sometimes disappointing those they feel called to serve, can take its toll. Many clergy struggle to hold appropriate boundaries and stretch themselves unreasonably; the practical and managerial aspects of the role can limit the space to nurture their own faith. (p. 21)

This summary well matches my experience from facilitating the Reflective Practice Group, and much of this is expressed through my quotes from my group notes included in the previous section on my own experience of the group. In the light of this powerful summary of the research in Clergy well-being, it is perhaps not surprising that I had a counter-transference reaction of feeling unhelpful. However, it is important to reiterate that the Clergy in my group did make good use of the group time; they did reflect on the challenges they faced; they did share their best ways of coping and their occasional good news items. My sense is that a Reflective Practice Group was not the total and complete response to these very real human challenges, and that an individually crafted response that could be adjusted over time, was probably the best way in supporting Clergy in their continuingly important work.

Final remarks

Not being a minister myself, meant that I had a (hopefully) quick learning curve on what being a minister involved, for my group participants. As previously mentioned, I have a number of ministers of various Christian, Jewish and Islamic faiths, as friends, colleagues and ex-students. However, I had not fully realised what was truly involved in their work. In addition, I became aware, during the course of these groups, of some unconscious notions of mine of what ministers stood for. Curiously, maybe even it was a form of synchronicity, my own faith journey was active in this time. I received some spiritual direction, had two deep and ongoing spiritual friendships and participated in both a Life and Faith group and a leaderless Spirituality group. In addition, I joined a new Church.

I was left wondering whether facilitation of such a group should only be done by a suitably trained minister. On balance, I think not, though joint facilitation with a minister might prove the best solution, practical issues aside. Facilitation by a minister might well prove different, but not necessarily better. For example, this would likely result in clarity around what was appropriate clerical behaviour and a shared ethical stance around practice. Gender may prove to be an issue in terms of who facilitates. With two facilitators, one could be a man, one a woman. I personally think that Reflective Practice Groups that are facilitated by ministers should not be facilitated by line managers of any of the clerics involved, and not be facilitated by anyone in the same ministerial area or diocese, to avoid possible role conflict.

As mentioned in the previous section, such groups should not be seen as the complete solution to any, and all, problems or challenges faced by ministers. In my view, what ministers need is an individually tailored choice of a mixture of further training, support, individual and peer supervision, and therapy/spiritual direction. This needs to be under regular review and the mix adjusted appropriately. The more stress they are under, the more support they will likely need.

Facilitating this Reflective Practice Group was not easy for me, which I think was an appropriate response. I was challenged in many ways by this experience, around issues of faith, and my understanding and appreciation of what ministry was, was made clearer and deepened. I remain full of admiration for the work of ministers.

As an academic, as a counsellor, and as a person of faith, I remain fascinated by our religious and spiritual journeys, and by the relationship between our faiths and the counselling encounter (West, 2017). I plan, in the near future, to build on my experience of facilitating this group by offering a somewhat similar group to people working in homeless hostels. This will be a different experience, as it will not necessarily have a religious aspect to it – although it may have if it is a Christian charity, and I do have some experience from my youth of working with homeless people.

CHAPTER EIGHT:
CONCLUDING REMARKS
Peter Madsen Gubi

Conclusion

During the writing of this book, the Covid-19 pandemic struck the world. Among all of the death and grief in the UK, Churches had to close their doors thus prohibiting a valuable source of comfort for many. Social distancing meant that ordinary ways of expressing compassion were embargoed. No more could Clergy offer a hug at a funeral. No more could those over 70 years of age attend a funeral, leaving families bereft, with Clergy stuck between feeling advanced empathy and having to maintain and monitor the social distancing rules. Some of the issues that presented themselves in Pastoral Supervision at the time were:

- Who am I now that I haven't got Church to fill my life with?;
- How do I embrace my reluctance at having to be exposed on social media, when I am intrinsically an introvert?;
- Why am I paying so much attention to the little bit of criticism on Facebook about my online services, when I am trying my best to adapt to a new reality? Don't they realise how difficult this is for me?;
- How do I now offer pastoral care effectively in these new circumstances?;
- How do I cope with the guilt of being in a 'vulnerable' category because of my health, whilst my parish expects me to take funerals and I can't?
- How does the gospel speak into situations of trauma within our community, and how do we continue to

offer a message of hope as a Church, without sounding like we are giving simplistic and pious answers that have no relevance to real life (like Job's friends did)?;

- How do I cope with my 'survivor's guilt' as I listen to the horrendous numbers of deaths, and to the traumatic impact that that has on families who are affected, whilst I am OK and relatively unscathed?;
- Who am I now that I can't offer the sacrament of Holy Communion?

The list of existential and practical issues goes on, which touch deeply into feelings of personal strife, suffering and inadequacy; and it is pertinent that many Clergy have had to face these kinds of difficult questions without the support of understanding others. Some have had to face these issues whilst also dealing with their own personal loss caused by the death of a loved one within their own family.

However, part of what the pandemic experience offered, was the opportunity to consider the implications of, and to experience, how Reflective Practice Groups could operate using technology, e.g. Zoom, WhatsApp, Skype, Microsoft Teams, etc. Although not quite 'the same' as meeting face-to-face, it has been our experience that they offer a 'good enough' platform for Reflective Practice Groups, without involving the travel. It may be that, post-pandemic, these internet platforms could be used in dioceses that are geographically challenged by the large area that they sometimes embrace. There is much to be gained from the reflective space created by journeying to, and from, the Reflective Practice Group, and of hosting the Reflective Practice Group in a place that is away from the day-to-day environment of each person. However, using internet platforms such as Zoom, WhatsApp, Skype, Microsoft Teams, etc., if more convenient for participants, are other ways of offering and enabling Reflective Practice Groups.

In this book, we have demonstrated that utilising Reflective Practice Groups supports Clergy well-being and formation, develops *phronesis* (i.e. insight and practical wisdom), and enables spiritual discernment and theological reflection to be developed in community. "By virtue of their calling, [pastors] need to nurture an ongoing and renewing relationship with God, to maintain life balance, reduce stress and avoid burnout" (Chandler, 2009, p. 284). Reflective Practice Groups provide participants with a safe place to "act from the centre" in order to "give God freedom in the world, to do the works of God" (Williams, 2000). They are also a form of Bonhoeffer's ecclesiology of "Christ existing as community" as both a form of 'Church' (i.e. Christian community), and as a place that enables and sustains "Church ... to be there for others, ... enabling the facilitation and articulation of limitations, struggles and failures" (McBride, 2014, pp. 92–95). Reflective Practice Groups are a helpful way of enabling reflective practice, developing a heart theology, and fostering good self-care practices for future ministry. Indeed, the future of the Church may depend on Clergy developing, and having, those skills.

REFERENCES

Awad, N. G. (2010). Personhood as particularity: John Zizioulas, Colin Gunton, and the Trinitarian theology of personhood. *Journal of Reformed Theology, 4*, 1–22.

Bagnall, S. (2000). *Clergy Support Groups: Evaluation of the pilot year.* Unpublished paper.

Barrett, J. (2010). *Living the practice: A research inquiry into clergy use of Reflective Practice Groups in the Exeter Diocese of the Church of England.* Unpublished MA dissertation: University of Middlesex, UK.

Becher, W. (1983). International Conferences on Pastoral Care. *The Journal of Pastoral Care, 37*(2), 122–126.

Bennett, Z. (2013). *Using the Bible in practical theology: Historical and contemporary perspectives.* Farnham, UK: Ashgate.

Benson, J. F. (1987). *Working more creatively in groups.* London, UK: Routledge.

Bolton, G. (2014). *Reflective practice: Writing and professional development* (4th ed.) London, UK: Sage Publications.

Bonhoeffer, D. (1954/2015). *Life together* (J. W. Doberstein, Trans., S. Wells, Foreword). London, UK: SCM Press.

Bonhoeffer, D. (1966). *Christology* (J. Bowden, Trans.). London, UK: Collins.

Braudaway-Bauman, C. (2012). Peer power: The promise of clergy support groups. *Christian Century, 11*, 22–25.

Braun, V., Clarke, V., & Rance, N. (2015). How to use thematic analysis with interview data. In A. Vossler & N. Moller (Eds.) *The counselling and psychotherapy research handbook* (pp. 843–860). London, UK: Sage Publications.

Bryant, D. (2004). *Chairs in a circle: A selection of papers in celebration of the Southwark Diocesan Group Scheme for Clergy and Pastoral Workers, 1970–2004.* Self-published booklet.

Bunton, P. (2001). *Cell groups and house Churches: What history teaches us.* Lititz, PA: House to House Publications.

Burton, J., & Burton, C. (2009). *Public people, private lives: Tackling stress in clergy families.* London, UK: Continuum.

Centre for Reflexive Theology. Retrieved from http://reflexivetheology.blogspot.co.uk/ [Accessed 7 January 2015].

Chandler, D. J. (2009). Pastoral burnout and the impact of personal spiritual renewal, rest-taking, and support system practices. *Journal of Pastoral Psychology, 58,* 273–287.

Charlton, H. (1997). *Collaborative research to explore values held by the members of Consultation and Support Groups.* Unpublished.

Charlton, R., Rolph, J., Francis, L. J., Rolph, P., & Robbins, M. (2009). Clergy work-related psychological health: Listening to the ministers of word and sacrament within the United Reformed Church in England. *Journal of Pastoral Psychology, 58,* 133–149.

Charry, E. T. (1997). *By the renewing of your minds: The pastoral function of Christian doctrine.* Oxford, UK: Oxford University Press.

Christian Research (2013). *Health concerns omnibus research – survey report.* Unpublished report for St Luke's Healthcare for the Clergy.

References

Church of England (2014). *Formation criteria with mapped selection criteria for ordained ministry in the Church of England.* Retrieved from https://www.churchofengland.org/media/ 2139103/formation criteria for ordained ministry approved hofbps dec 2014.docx

Craddock, F. B. (2002). *Overhearing the Gospel.* St. Louis, MO: Chalice.

Crisp, O. D. (2005). Problems with Perichoresis. *Tyndale Bulletin, 56*(1), 119–140.

Crouter, R. (2005). Shaping an academic discipline: The brief outline on the study of theology. In J. Marina (Ed.). *The Cambridge companion to Friedrich Schleiermacher* (pp. 111–128). Cambridge, UK: Cambridge University Press.

Davies, O. (2013). *Theology of transformation: Faith, freedom, and the Christian Act.* Oxford, UK: Oxford University Press.

Denniston, J. (2014). Theory into Practice: A challenge for supervisors in formation for ordained ministry. In M. Paterson & J. Rose (Eds.), *Enriching ministry: Pastoral supervision in practice* (pp. 105-118). London, UK: SCM Press.

Diocese of Chelmsford (2006). *Clergy Support Groups: A resource of CME to the Diocese of Chelmsford.* Report to CME and the Bishop's Staff. Unpublished paper.

Diocese of Glasgow and Galloway (2012). Retrieved from http://md.glasgow.anglican.org/wp-content/ uploads/2011/09/2012-2013-CMD-Handbook.pdf

Diocese of Salisbury (2015). *Reflective Practice Groups for Clergy: The philosophy and practice of clergy working together in groups.* Unpublished Briefing Paper.

Diocese of Salisbury Ministry Development Team (2005). *Work-Based Learning Groups in Action: The history, philosophy and rationale of clergy working together in groups*. Unpublished Briefing Paper.

Diocese of Worcester (2020). *A Reflective Practice Group for Clergy*. Retrieved from https://cofeworcester.contentfiles.net/media/assets/file/1418_CofE_BalintA5_4pp2019_4.pdf [Accessed 25 April 2020].

Dominian, J. (1998). *One like us: A psychological interpretation of Jesus*. London, UK: Darton, Longman and Todd.

Donahue, B., & Robinson, R. (2001). *Building a Church of small groups: A place where nobody stands alone*. Grand Rapids, MI: Zondervan.

Donati, M., & Watts, M. (2005). Personal development in counsellor training: Towards a clarification of inter-related concepts. *British Journal of Guidance and Counselling, 33*(4), 475–484.

Dryden, W., Horton, I., & Mearns, D. (1995). *Issues in Professional Counselling*. London, UK: Cassell.

Ellis, G. F. R. (2001). Kenosis as a unifying theme for life and cosmology. In J. Polkinghorne (Ed.), *The Work of Love* (pp. 107–126). London, UK: SPCK.

Faull, K. (2011). Instructions for body and soul: 18th Century Moravian care of the self. *The Hinge: International Theological Dialog for the Moravian Church, 18*(2), 3–28.

Fiddes, P. S. (2000). *Participating in God: A pastoral doctrine of the Trinity*. London, UK: Darton, Longman and Todd.

Foster, C. R., Dahill, L. E., Goleman, L. A., & Wang Tolentino, B. (2006). *Educating clergy: Teaching practices and pastoral imagination*. San Francisco, CA: Jossey-Bass.

References

Francis, L. J. (2018). Healthy leadership: The science of clergy work-related psychological health. In R. Brouwer (Ed.), *The future of lived religious leadership* (pp. 116–134). Amsterdam, Netherlands: VU University Press.

Francis, L. J., Robbins, M., & Wulff, K. (2013). Assessing the effectiveness of support strategies in reducing professional burnout among clergy serving in the Presbyterian Church (USA). *Practical Theology Journal*, *6*(3), 319–331.

Freeman, A. J. (1998). *An ecumenical theology of the heart: The theology of Count Nicholas Ludwig von Zinzendorf.* Bethlehem, PA: The Moravian Church in America.

General Synod (2019). *GS2133 Covenant for clergy care and well-being: Executive summary.* Retrieved from https://www.churchofengland.org/sites/default/files/2019-06/GS%202133%20A%20Covenant%20for%20Clergy%20Care%20and%20Well-being.pdf [Accessed 24 April 2020]

Graf, L. (2012). Learning from our past: Ideas for a 21st century choir system. *The Hinge: International Theological Dialog for the Moravian Church, 18*(3), 2–12.

Graham, E., Walton, H., & Ward. F. (2005). *Theological reflection: Methods.* London, UK: SCM Press.

Graham, E., Walton, H., & Ward. F. (2007). *Theological reflection: Sources.* London, UK: SCM Press.

Green, C. J. (1999). *Bonhoeffer: A theology of sociality.* Grand Rapids, MI: Eerdmans.

Gubi, P. M. (2008). *Prayer in counselling and psychotherapy: Exploring a hidden, meaningful dimension.* London, UK: Jessica Kingsley.

Gubi, P. M. (2009). A qualitative exploration into how the use of prayer in counselling and psychotherapy might be ethically problematic. *Counselling and Psychotherapy Research, 9*(2), 114–120.

Gubi, P. M. (2011). An exploration of the impact of small spiritually reflexive groups on personal and spiritual development. *Practical Theology Journal, 4*(1), 49–66.

Gubi, P. M. (2015). The importance of relationship. In P. M. Gubi (Ed.), *Spiritual Counselling: Journeying with Psyche and Soul.* London, UK & New York, NY: Jessica Kingsley Publishers.

Gubi, P. M. (2016). Assessing the perceived value of reflexive groups for supporting clergy in the Church of England. *Journal of Mental Health, Religion and Culture, 19*(4), 350–361.

Gubi, P. M. (2017). Assessing the perceived limitations of reflexive groups for supporting clergy in the Church of England. *Journal of Mental Health, Religion and Culture, 19*(7), 769–780.

Gubi, P. M. (2019). Utilising Reflective Practice Groups as pedagogy in ordination training and theological development. *Practical Theology Journal, 12*(4), 366–378.

Gubi, P. M. (2020). Exploring the impact, value and limitations of Reflective Practice Groups for Clergy in a Church in Wales diocese. *Journal of Mental Health, Religion and Culture,*
https://doi.org/10.1080/13674676.2020.1789571

Gubi, P. M., & Korris, J. (2015). Supporting Church of England Clergy through the provision of Reflective Practice Groups. *Thresholds: The Journal of BACP Spirituality Division.* Winter, 20–24.

References

Gunton, C. (1993). *The one, the three and the many: God, creation and the culture of modernity.* London & Cambridge, UK: Cambridge University Press.

Gunton, C. (1997). *Yesterday and today* (2nd ed.). London, UK: SPCK.

Hall, E., Hall, C., Harris, B., Hay, D., Biddulph, M., & Duffy, T. (1999). An evaluation of the long-term outcomes of small group work for counsellor development. *British Journal of Guidance and Counselling, 27*(1), 99–112.

Harkness, A. (2012). Learning approaches in theological education institutions: Faculty and student expectations in a South Asian Seminary. *The Journal of Adult Theological Education, 9*(2), 139–157.

Heriot, J. (2010). 'Spiritual but not religious': How small groups in America redefine religion. In J. F. Maynard, L. Hummel, & M. C. Moschella, (Eds.), *Pastoral bearings: Lived religion and pastoral theology* (pp. 179–210). New York, NY: Lexington Books.

Houston, S. (2015). *Reflective Practice: A model for Supervision and Practice in Social Work.* Belfast, UK: Northern Ireland Social Care Council.

Hudson, R. (2015). Is there a need for specialist counselling for church ministers? *Thresholds: The Journal of BACP Spirituality.* Autumn: 10–13.

Hurding, R. F. (1985). *Roots and shoots: A guide to counselling and psychotherapy.* London, UK: Hodder and Stoughton.

Ison, H. (2020a). Working with an embodied and systemic approach to trauma and tragedy. In M. Warner, C. Southgate, C. A. Grosh-Miller, & H. Ison, (Eds.), *Tragedies and Christian congregations: The practical theology of trauma* (pp. 47–63). London, UK: Routledge.

Ison, H. (2020b). *Thoughts from a trauma-informed perspective on the Covid-19 crisis.* Retrieved from https://llandaff.churchinwales.org.uk/wp-content/uploads/sites/5/2020/04/Thoughts-from-a-trauma-informed-perspective.pdf [Accessed 25 April 2020]

Ixer, G. (1999). There's no such thing as reflection. *British Journal of Social Work, 29*(4), 513–527.

Ixer, G. (2010). There's no such thing as reflection: Ten years on. *The Journal of Practice Teaching in Health and Social Work, 10*(1), 75–93.

Jackson-Jordan, E. A. (2013). Clergy burnout: A review of the literature, *Journal of Pastoral Care and Counselling, 67*(1), 1–5.

Jaques, D., & Salaman, G. (2006). *Learning in groups.* London, UK: Routledge.

Johns, H. (2012). *Personal development in counsellor training* (2nd ed.). London, UK: Sage Publications.

Kelly, E. (2012). *Personhood and presence: Self as a resource for spiritual and pastoral care.* London, UK: Bloomsbury.

Kelly, E. (2013). Translating theological reflective practice into values based reflection: A report from Scotland. *Reflective practice: Formation and supervision in ministry. 33,* 245–256.

Kelly, E. (2014). Risking the embodied self: A theology of presence in pastoral supervision. In M. Paterson & J. Rose (Eds.), *Enriching ministry: Pastoral supervision in practice* (pp. 40–52). London, UK: SCM Press.

Kilby, K. (2000). Perichoresis and projection: Problems with social doctrines of the Trinity. *New Blackfriars, 81*(957), 432–445.

Kinast, R. L. (1996). *Let ministry teach: A guide to theological reflection.* Collegeville, MN: Liturgical Press.

References

Ladd, N. (2014). Theological education at the crossroads. *Dialog: A Journal of Theology*, *53*(4), 356–364.

Leach, J., & Paterson, M. (2015). *Pastoral supervision: A handbook* (2nd ed.). London, UK: SCM Press.

Lee, C., & Horsman, S. (2002). *Affirmation and accountability*. Exeter, UK: The Society of Martha and Mary.

Lennie, C. (2007). The role of Personal Development Groups in counsellor training: Understanding factors contributing to self-awareness in the Personal Development Group. *British Journal of Guidance and Counselling*, *35*(1), 115–129.

Lieberman, M. A. (1983). Comparative analysis of change mechanisms in groups. In H. H. Blumberg, A. P. Hare, V. Kent, & M. Davies (Eds.), *Small groups and social interaction* (pp. 239–252). London, UK: Wiley.

Lyall, D. (2009). 'Supervision as ministry'. *Practical Theology*, *2*(3), 317–325.

Macquarrie, J. (1974). Kenoticism reconsidered. *Theology*, *LXVII*, 115–124.

Mahoney, J. (2000). The moral context of pastoral care. *Contact Pastoral Monograph*, 10. Edinburgh, UK: Contact.

McBride, J. M. (2014). Christ existing as concrete community today, *Theology Today*, *7*(1), 92–105.

McCallum, D., & Lowery, J. (2012). *Organic discipleship: Mentoring others into spiritual maturity and leadership*. New York, NY: New Paradigm Publishing.

McDougall, J. A. (2005). *Pilgrimage of love: Moltmann on the Trinity and Christian life*. Oxford, UK: Oxford University Press.

McFadyen, A. I. (1990). *The call to personhood*. Cambridge, UK: Cambridge University Press.

McLeod, J. (2009). *An introduction to counselling* (4th ed.). Maidenhead, UK: Open University Press.

McLeod, J., & McLeod, J. (2014). *Personal and professional development for counsellors, psychotherapists and mental health practitioners*. Buckingham, UK: Open University Press.

Mearns, D. (1997). *Person-centred counselling training*. London, UK: Sage Publications.

Methodist Church (2017). *Responsible Grace: Supervising in the Methodist Church*. London, UK: The Methodist Church.

Miles, A., & Proeschold-Bell, R. J. (2013). Overcoming the challenges of pastoral work? Peer Support Groups and psychological distress among United Methodist Church Clergy. *Sociology of Religion, 74*(2), 199–226.

Ministry Division (2019). *Ministerial Effectiveness and well-being: Exploring the flourishing of clergy and ordinands*. London, UK: The Archbishops' Council of the Church of England.

Moltmann, J. (1973). *Theology and joy*. London, UK: SCM Press.

Moltmann, J. (1981). *The Trinity and the Kingdom of God* (M. Khol Trans.). London, UK: SCM Press.

Moon, J. (2004). *A handbook of reflective and experiential learning: Theory and practice*. London, UK: Routledge.

Mullally, B. (2017). The effect of presence and power in the pastoral supervisory relationship. *HOLINESS: The Journal of Wesley House Cambridge, 3*(1), 5–34.

Nash, P., & Nash, S. (2009). *Tools for reflective ministry*. London, UK: SPCK.

Nash, S. (2002). *Supporting urban youth workers*. Unpublished DMin thesis. University of Sheffield, UK.

Nash, S. (2011). Regenerative practice. *Reflective Practice, 12*(3), 427–238.

References

Oakley, L., & Kinmond, K. (2013). *Breaking the silence on spiritual abuse*. Basingstoke, UK: Palgrave Macmillan.

Oakley, L., & Humphreys, J. (2019). *Escaping the maze of spiritual abuse: Creating healthy Christian cultures*. London, UK: SPCK.

Otto, R. E. (2001). The use and abuse of perichoresis in recent theology. *Scottish Journal of Theology*, 54(3): 366–384.

Payne, H. (1999). Personal Development Groups in the training of counsellors and therapists: A review of the research. *European Journal of Psychotherapy, Counselling and Health*, 2(1): 55–68.

Payne, H. (2001). Student experiences in a personal development group: The question of safety. *European Journal of Psychotherapy, Counselling and Health*, 4(2), 267–292.

Podmore, C. (1998). *The Moravian Church in England: 1728–1760*. Oxford, UK: Oxford University Press.

Preston-Shoot, M. (2007). *Effective group work* (2nd ed.). London, UK: Macmillan.

Pryce, R. M. (2014). *The poetry of priesthood: A study of the contribution of poetry to the continuing ministerial education of clergy in the Church of England*. Unpublished DPT thesis: University of Birmingham, UK.

Pryce, R. M. (2019). *Poetry, practical theology and reflective practice*. London, UK: Routledge.

Reiss, R. (2013). *The testing of vocation: 100 years of ministry selection in the Church of England*. London, UK: Church House Publishing.

Rhymes, D. (1993). *Time past to time future*. London, UK: Darton, Longman and Todd.

Robson, M., & Robson, J. (2009). Explorations of participants' experiences of a Personal Development Group held as part of a counselling psychology training group: Is it safe here? *Counselling Psychology Quarterly*, *21*(4), 371–382.

Rogers, C. R. (1980). *A way of being*. New York, NY: Houghton Mifflin.

Rose, C. (2008). *The Personal Development Group: The students' guide*. London, UK: Karnac Books.

Rose, C. (Ed.). (2012). *Self-awareness and personal development: Resources for psychotherapists and counsellors*. Basingstoke, UK: Palgrave Macmillan.

Rowell, P. C., & Benshoff, J. M. (2008). Using personal growth groups in multicultural counselling courses to foster students' ethnic identity development. *Counsellor Education and Supervision*, *48*, 2–15.

Schleiermacher, F. (1977). *Hermeneutics: The handwritten manuscripts* (H. Kimmerle, [Ed.], J. Duke, & J. Forstman, [Trans.]). Missoula, MT: Scholars Press.

Schmid, P. F. (2006). *In the beginning there is community: Implications and challenges of the belief in a triune God and a person-centred approach*. Norwich, UK: The Norwich Centre.

Schön, D. (1984). *The reflective practitioner: How professionals think in action*. New York, NY: Basic Books.

Siegel, B., & Donnelly, J. C. (1978). Enriching personal and professional development: The experience of a support group for interns. *Journal of Medical Education*, *53*, 908–914.

Sims, N. (2011). Theologically reflective practice: A key tool for contemporary ministry. *Reflective Practice: Formation and Supervision in Ministry*, *31*, 166–176.

References

Smith, J. A., Flowers, P., & Larkin, M. (2009). *Interpretive Phenomenological Analysis: Theory, method and research.* London, UK: Sage Publications.

Stuart-White, B., Vaughan-Wilson, J., Eatock, J., Muskett, J. A., & Village, A. (2018). Isolation among rural Clergy: Exploring experiences and solutions in one diocese. *Rural Theology, 1*(2), 65–79.

Swinton, J. (2018). *Raging with compassion: Pastoral responses to the problem of evil.* London, UK: SCM Press.

Taylor, J. (1972). *The go-between God: The Holy Spirit and Christian Mission.* London, UK: SCM Press.

The Archbishops' Council of the Church of England (2003). *Formation for ministry within a learning church: The structure and funding of ordination training. A summary of the report* [GS Misc 710]. London, UK: Church House Publishing.

Thompson, S., & Thompson, N. (2008). *The critically reflective practitioner.* Basingstoke, UK: Palgrave Macmillan.

Thorne, B. (2002). *The mystical power of Person-Centred Therapy: Hope beyond despair.* London, UK: Whurr Publishers.

Travis, M. (2008). Supporting Clergy in postmodern ministry. *Practical Theology Journal, 1*(1), 95–130.

Volf, M. (1998). *After our likeness: The Church as the image of the Trinity.* Grand Rapids, MI: Eerdmans.

Walrond-Skinner, S. (n.d.). *Diocese of Southwark Consultation and Support Groups.* Unpublished paper.

Walton, H. (2014). *Writing methods in theological reflection.* London, UK: SCM Press.

Ward, F. (2005). *Lifelong learning: Theological education and supervision.* London, UK: SCM Press.

Watson, K. M. (2010). Forerunners of the early Methodist Band Meeting. *Methodist Review: A Journal of Wesleyan and Methodist Studies*, 2, 1–31.

Weinlick, J. R. (2001). *Count Zinzendorf: The story of his life and leadership in the renewed Moravian Church*. Bethlehem, PA: The Moravian Church in America.

West, W. (2017). Counsellors and religious pastoral carers in dialogue. In P. M. Gubi, (Ed.). *What counsellors and spiritual directors can learn from each other* (pp. 157–167). London, UK: Jessica Kingsley.

Whipp, M. (2019). Theological essay. In General Synod (2019). *GS2133 Covenant for Clergy Care and Well-being: Executive summary*. Retrieved from https://www.churchofengland.org/sites/default/files/2019-06/GS%202133%20A%20Covenant%20for%20Clergy%20Care%20and%20Wellbeing.pdf [Accessed 24 April 2020].

Williams, D. I., & Irving, J. A. (1996). Personal growth: Rogerian paradoxes. *British Journal of Guidance and Counselling*. 24(2), 165–172.

Williams, R. (2000). *On Christian theology*. Oxford, UK: Blackwell Publishing.

Wolfe, D. M., & Kolb, D. A. (1980). Career development, personal growth, and experiential learning. In D. A. Kolb, I. Rubin, & J. McIntyre, (Eds.), *Organisation psychology: A book of readings* (pp. 124–152). Upper Saddle River, NJ: Prentice Hall Publishing.

Zeckhausen, W. A. (1997). Pastoral counselor-led Physician Support Groups. *American Journal of Pastoral Counseling*, 1(1), 61–74.

Zizioulas, J. D. (1985). *Being as communion*. London, UK: Darton, Longman and Todd.